THE STORY OF THE MIRACLES AT
COOKIE'S TABLE
BY WESLEY ENOCH

CURRENCY PRESS
The performing arts publisher
www.currency.com.au

GRIFFIN
THEATRE COMPANY

Principal Sponsor
PKF
Chartered Accountants
& Business Advisers

CURRENCY PLAYS

First published in 2007
by Currency Press Pty Ltd,
PO Box 2287, Strawberry Hills, NSW, 2012, Australia
enquiries@currency.com.au
www.currency.com.au
in association with
Griffin Theatre Company, Sydney
Reprinted 2015, 2021.
NATIONAL LIBRARY OF AUSTRALIA CIP DATA

Enoch, Wesley, 1961–.
The story of the miracles at Cookie's table.
ISBN 9780868198033 (pbk.).
1. Women, Aboriginal Australian – Drama. 2. Family – Drama. I. Title.
A822.3

Typeset by Dean Nottle for Currency Press.
Front cover shows Leah Purcell as Annie in the 2007 Griffin Theatre
Company/ HotHouse Theatre production. (Photo: Mark Rogers)

Contents

Currency Press acknowledges the Traditional Owners of the Country on which we live and work. We pay our respects to all Aboriginal and Torres Strait Islander Elders, past and present.

The Story of the Miracles at Cookie's Table was first produced by Griffin Theatre Company and HotHouse Theatre at the SBW Stables Theatre, Sydney, on 15 August 2007 with the following cast:

ANNIE	Leah Purcell
FAITH	Roxanne McDonald
NATHAN	Russell Smith
YOUNG NATHAN	Ben Dennison / Blake Herczeg

Director, Marion Potts
Designer, Bruce McKinven
Lighting Designer, Luiz Pampolha
Composer / Sound Designer, Brett Collery

ACKNOWLEDGEMENTS

Thanks to:

Aboriginal and Torres Strait Islander Arts Board of the Australia Council for the three-month residency in Paris at the Cité Internationale des Arts.

Sue Street for the week of escape in Hong Kong.

My family and my Nana, who everyone called Cookie.

Stephen Armstrong for helping me through some hard bits in my life.

HotHouse Theatre for picking up the commission and providing a month in the country.

Ilbijerri for assisting with a reading and workshop in December 2003 as part of the third Victorian Indigenous Playwrights' Conference.

The 2005 ANPC Conference for the reading.

The Sydney Theatre Company and *Sydney Morning Herald* for selecting it for the Patrick White Playwriting Award.

Yoshio Wada, Sudo Rei and Sawada-San for the marvellous translation into Japanese and the premiere production in Tokyo by Rakutendan Theatre Company 2006.

Dramaturgical support: Campion Decent, Hilary Glow, Jan McKemmish, Peter Matheson, Aidan Fennessey and the Artistic Directorate and staff of Hothouse Theatre, and the cast and crew of the 2007 production.

WRITER'S NOTE

At the centre of this play is a table and a few chairs. Though all the action happens in a naturalistic kitchen, it isn't meant to be a naturalistic play. The table is the constant, we are able to change time periods at will, characters slip from one time period to another easily re-living and enacting memories, though we always return to the present day. A change in tone can be marked by snaps of lights and/or sounds, some elements may extend through two time periods—for example, a storm is happening in 1950s and in the present day—and the two time periods are enacted simultaneously.

This play is about storytelling and how stories bind us together as families. All the different half-memories and versions of an event help to write our history in the absence of a clear literary record. *Cookie's Table* is a metaphor for culture lived, lost, found, obscured and metamorphosed into a hybrid reality for contemporary Murri people. The unbroken line of cultural practices, through the feeding and gathering of our families around the table, is as much a sign of our cultural continuity as any anthropological data gathered in the middens, caves and campsites of our forebears. In these days of Native Title and the need to prove ourselves, *Cookie's Table* is a story about the strength of family, adapting and gathering together.

PUNCTUATION

To guide the rhythm I have used different punctuation to indicate different things:
    … to indicate a trailing-off of thought
    ( ) to indicate the words the character is thinking, which may or
        may not need to be spoken
    — a change or break of thought
    / a quick, almost seamless change of thought

CHARACTERS

NATHAN, an Aboiriginal man in his mid-30s, a well-dressed, well-educated and well-presented professional

YOUNG NATHAN, aged 10-12

ANNIE, his mother, late 40s/early 50s, stylish, likes to be the centre of attention, joker, a singer

FAITH, her mother, early 70s, church-hardened woman, family matriarch, the great provider

Note: This play went to press before the end of rehearsals, so may differ slighly from the play as performed.

ACT ONE

SCENE ONE

The sound of women singing.

A man in his mid-thirties enters. This is NATHAN. *He is dressed in suit and overcoat. There is a heaviness in his walk. He goes to the table and chairs sitting in the middle of the room and sits down. He looks to the audience.*

NATHAN: This is the story of Cookie's Table.

Cookie was my great, great grandmother. And this table has been passed down the generations, from Cookie to her daughter Kawana to my Nana Faith, and now to me.

The story goes something like this… When my great, great grandmother was born, it was under a tree—a tree her mother had chosen. We believe the tree you're born under gives you something… like part of its spirit—and this tree was chosen 'cause it was strong with a wide trunk, yet supple enough to bend in the wind to survive fierce storms… While her mother held onto a branch surrounded by her aunts, my great, great grandmother was born.

The story goes that my great, great grandmother spent the first years of her life learning all about the island and the ocean. How to fish and cook everything from the sea—dugong and turtle, whiting and eugaries… and even at a young age the older women would bring her things to cook. She had a knack for putting foods together in a way which made them taste better. This was her island, her home.

When the white men came it didn't stop her, she cooked and hunted as she had always done. She'd watch the ships coming and going but didn't think anything of it. But when they cut down her birth tree, she felt it… like something had been torn out of her. She was in a canoe out on the bay fishing, and she felt like something had hooked her in the chest, was pulling her in, reeling her back to the shore. She went straight to the place—the stump where it had once stood. She followed the tracks where the log had been dragged and in the pile of dead trees at the bottom of the hill she found it—gutted. She followed the log and watched it made into lumber, tracking it until she knew exactly where it was. In the kitchen.

ANNIE *appears and* NATHAN *fades away.*

ANNIE: The story goes something like this… Cookie worked in that kitchen and lived there in the house. Cleaning mostly—but when the whitefella cook got crook one day, she was left to feed the house. This young one—maybe fifteen, but in them days that was old enough to be a woman—this young one left to cook for officers and convicts and soldiers. [*With a smile*] And that day she cooked up the biggest feed and, if you believe the stories, she did that loaves and fishes thing, feeding thirty men with half a pound of flour, a lump of meat and some stale tea. The men reckoned that cook fella could go get stuffed 'cause no way they were going back to his shitty food after they'd tasted Cookie's meal. That cook fella got all gooly up and rowed hisself back to the mainland. She was it from then on—and even later when other women came to live in that house—Cookie ran that kitchen. She'd only wanted to be close to her beginning place, her birth tree. She was young and beautiful and eventually caught the eye of a young army fella, white one. She'd be cooking in the house and before the washing up was finished she would steal away with him to walk the sand dunes and watch the whales swimming down the coast.

We don't know who her mother was, if she had sisters or what other family. It gets to the point you have no need for more family than you have stories for.

ANNIE *sings a lullaby.* FAITH *appears.*

FAITH: The story goes… He filled her head with his language and her tummy with his children. She believed his dreams and in return she forgot her own. She gave him a son whom he named Nathaniel after his father. He would talk rubbish about them going to South Africa when he got a promotion. How their son would be educated in a good school. A year later their daughter was born, Kawana, and he took no interest in her. She was my mother. This soldier fella did not take Cookie as his wife and he heaped sin upon her soul. Cookie, desperate for his love, gave him another son whom he named Jason after himself. These three children… dark, coffee-coloured children with wavy hair and green eyes, lived with their mother all in the same bed and when their father came to her in the night they would sleep under the table in the kitchen. When his promotion finally came through, he was full of regrets and wept genuine tears for his sons. The dreams of a good school and a different life now whistled with a hollow wind. This is the earliest story of my family. This is the beginning of Cookie's Table.

◆ ◆ ◆ ◆ ◆

SCENE TWO: PRESENT DAY

NATHAN *sits at the table. A middle-aged woman enters. This is* ANNIE. *She's dressed in black, stylish. She carries her shoes. She's been drinking. She enters singing 'Bringing in the Sheaves'.*

NATHAN: Where did you get to?

ANNIE: I was catching up with your uncle Clay, I haven't seen him in…

NATHAN: I've been waiting.

ANNIE: 'Course, son.

NATHAN: I can't hang around all night.

ANNIE: I haven't seen half that lot… (for ages.)

NATHAN: I want the table.

> *Silence.*

ANNIE: You look a lot like your uncle Clay (you know that?)

NATHAN: Did you hear me?

> *Silence.*

ANNIE: That lovely thick hair, strong nose and your crinkled up forehead, you could be brothers.

NATHAN: Mum! I want the table.

ANNIE: So I'm still your mother, am I? I thought you'd forgotten.

NATHAN: You can keep everything else.

> *Silence.*

ANNIE: Come on and have a charge with your mother.

NATHAN: You know I can't.

ANNIE: Come on, the barge doesn't leave for another half hour. Just sit down with me for a little while.

NATHAN: Annie, I can't…

ANNIE: So I'm Annie again, am I?

NATHAN: Mum, I can't—be with you—when you're like… this.

ANNIE: Like what? Your grandmother's not cold in her grave and you're begrudging me a little drink.

> NATHAN*'s mobile phone rings. He stands up and walks away, answering it very business-like. Though he speaks Japanese, we hear the word 'Prime Minister' very clearly.*

NATHAN: [*into the phone*] Yes. [*The rest is in Japanese.*] Hello, so sorry to have kept you waiting… Yes, yes… Yes thank you, I received your flowers… No not yet, I expect to be back tomorrow morning. The Prime Minister will be very glad for your concern. Thank you. [*He hangs up. In English*] Mum. I have to go.

ANNIE: So you keep saying. Now sit down.

NATHAN: I ordered a water taxi.

ANNIE: (Oh.) The government must be paying.

NATHAN: If I leave now I can catch the last flight to Sydney.

ANNIE: The last flight to Sydney. [*Laughing*] I remember when you couldn't even wipe your own arse. Sit down and talk to me.

> *Pause.*

NATHAN: Will you give me the table?

> NATHAN *glances at his watch and then sits down at the table again.*

ANNIE: When you were born. Your grandmother tried to talk me out of going to the hospital. She told me that story about giving birth under the tree and I said to her, 'I thought you were meant to *make* babies under a tree. Shit, I wouldn't have spent all that time getting bark rash.'

> NATHAN *gets up as if to leave.*

Sit down. I promise no more jokes. [*Pause.*] I haven't been much of a mother to you. [*Close to tears*] She had her bad side too, you know. But now she's gone, we can be a family again. It's not too late to be a mother, properly. There's lots of women just having kids at my age.

NATHAN: No there isn't.

ANNIE: What?

NATHAN: Don't worry.

ANNIE: Women in their early forties are having kids all the time.

NATHAN: You aren't in your early forties.

ANNIE: (Of course I am.) Don't be stupid. I know how old I am.

NATHAN: I'm thirty-five.

ANNIE: Are you? What year were you born?

NATHAN: You were there (weren't you?)

ANNIE: I was very young…

NATHAN: I know… I just want to know about the table.

ANNIE: It was a nice service. I remember a time when fire and brimstone were the only things talked about in that church.

NATHAN: Annie. The table.

ANNIE: Faithie left everything to me. She did.

NATHAN: Nana left everything to you 'cause she knew you had nothing.

ANNIE: It's a family heirloom, this table. Been passed down from my grandmother to my mother and now to me. It might be very valuable…

NATHAN: Is this what we're talking about? How much do you want? Two thousand? Three thousand? Ten thousand? I should have known… why don't I just give you the cheque and you can fill it in.

ANNIE: Who said anything… (about money?)

NATHAN: Just write in how much you want.

ANNIE: Do I look desperate?

NATHAN: Just take the money then this can be finished with.

NATHAN *signs a cheque and leaves it on the table.*

ANNIE: That's how you deal with family now, is it? Send a cheque so you don't have to talk with us no more. Oh, that's good that is. 'Oh, it's Christmas—send them a cheque—that'll keep them off my back for another year.' You hang around with those gubberment people long enough and you become one, you know that. Just hand out the money, don't ask what the problem is, just throw some bungoo at them and let them fight amongst themselves.

NATHAN: What do you want?

ANNIE: I just want you to sit down and talk with your mother for a little while. (That too much to ask?)

NATHAN *sits down at the table.*

NATHAN: Annie. When the taxi calls, I'm going.

ANNIE: I speak English. Not like you, I reckon you just make it up… [*She mockingly speaks Japanese.*] We beat them you know… in Vietnam… we beat them

NATHAN: Wrong war, wrong language.

ANNIE: What?

NATHAN: It's Japanese. World War Two.

ANNIE: What's the diff? They're all the same. We beat all them lot!

NATHAN: What?

ANNIE: I did my bit for my country. I helped out.

NATHAN: You were a singer/

ANNIE: [*beating her chest*] I entertained the troupes, I did my bit.

NATHAN: In a club in South Brisbane.

ANNIE: That's overseas.

NATHAN: Okay. Okay, you did your bit!

> *Flashback:* FAITH *appears as an echo of another time.*
>
> ANNIE, *in the present day, sits bolt upright.*

FAITH: If you walk out that door, God help you, you won't be coming back here. Do you hear me, Annie? Annie? Annie? Annie. You'll never be happy if you leave this island. Do you hear me, you'll never be happy.

> *Back to the present day.*
>
> *Silence.*

ANNIE: This table meant a lot to her. She said it was the secret to her cooking. I tried cooking the same meals wherever I was, but they never tasted the same as hers. I used the same recipes and everything. She said it was the table that did it, made it different.

> *Flashback:* FAITH *appears as an echo of another time.*

FAITH: This table's got proper history in it. A hundred years of damper making, a hundred years of chopping and love, a hundred years of yarning and cups of tea. That's what makes it special… you can't get that at McDonald's.

> *Back to the present day.*

ANNIE: She was beautiful when she was young. She had my bones and she wore her hair in that way that was real stylish. She'd let me comb it. And we'd sit around and talk 'til all hours, just her and me. She'd tell me things just for me/ things I couldn't tell you about/ Things her mother told her, proper tribal things about the lakes and the sand ridge and the bay and how to cook with respect for the thing that had given its life for you to eat. (I was too young to understand.)

◆ ◆ ◆ ◆ ◆

SCENE THREE: 1979

FAITH *enters with* YOUNG NATHAN, *aged ten. They sit at the table. She is carrying a wad of mail.*

FAITH: So she was born under the tree…

YOUNG NATHAN: And they chopped it down and built a house with a kitchen and she went and worked in that kitchen so she could be close to that tree.

FAITH: And when it came time to have her babies, she had them in that kitchen on that table, with the wood stove burning hot, didn't matter if it was summer or winter/

YOUNG NATHAN: First her son and then her daughter and then another son.

FAITH: She named the boys Nathaniel and Jason and her daughter she called Kawana which means the calm waters. Kawana was my mother, your…

YOUNG NATHAN: great grandmother. Can I have brothers, too?

FAITH: No, Nathan.

YOUNG NATHAN: But everyone has brothers and sisters.

FAITH: No.

YOUNG NATHAN: When I'm older, can I have a brother?

FAITH: When you're older you'll see why that's a silly thing to ask.

YOUNG NATHAN: I want to see now.

FAITH: What are you in a hurry for? Only rushing to your grave. [*Pause.*] The Lord created you special, you're a one of a kind.

    She kisses him.

Now… off you scoot to bed. I'll be in soon to brush your hair.

    YOUNG NATHAN *exits.*

◆ ◆ ◆ ◆ ◆

SCENE FOUR: 1991

FAITH: God works in mysterious ways.

> *The faint sound of a kookaburra.* FAITH *looks through the letters and takes out a postcard, sees it's from Annie and puts it into the table drawer. She looks at another letter.*
>
> *Change of time.* NATHAN *watches from the sidelines.*

FAITH: Nathan! Nathan! It's here!! Look here... the coat of arms... it has to be it... It's addressed to you. Naaaathan!

> FAITH *puts her glasses on as she sits down.*

You've prayed about this, then? Whatever it says will be God's will... And you've tried your hardest? Patience now... [*She slowly opens the letter*] It's just like the Oscars. [*She takes out the letter and reads it.*] 'Dear Mr Yeoman,'—oh that's nice, isn't it?—'Thank you for your application...' [*Mumble, mumble, mumble*] 'We congratulate you on your outstanding results... However, we believe you to be inappropriate for our Aboriginal Recruitment Scheme...' I'm sorry, love. [*Reading*] '... inappropriate for our Aboriginal Recruitment Scheme... and have recommended you for our Mainstream Graduate Program with a placement in the Department of Foreign Affairs and Trade'... What does that mean?

NATHAN: It means I'm in.

FAITH: But what do they mean you're inappropriate? But you are Aboriginal... what does this mean you're inappropriate? You got into that University course through the Aborigines entry and your grades were really good then. Maybe you shouldn't do it... they think you're not Murri enough/ It doesn't feel right. You'll be so far away. Away from the other Murris?

NATHAN: It doesn't matter how I get in... I'm in.

> *Silence.*

FAITH: God works in mysterious ways.

◆ ◆ ◆ ◆ ◆

SCENE FIVE: PRESENT DAY

NATHAN's *phone rings. A groaning sound is heard offstage.* NATHAN *looks at his watch as he talks.*

NATHAN: [*into the phone*] Hello.... Jesus... Well, this is great... Yes, yes, yes, yes yes... Well, the sooner the better. Call me when you're close.

    He hangs up and puts the phone on the table. He rubs his chest.

    ANNIE *appears groaning and wiping her chin, she's been throwing up in the bathroom.*

If you ate something before you started drinking you wouldn't get sick.

ANNIE: If I ate something before I started drinking it'd just hurt when I chucked it up/ Since when did I start taking advice from a teetotaller?— [*Pause.*] Was that your water taxi?

NATHAN: They're expecting a storm.

ANNIE: [*with a little smile of victory*] Well/

NATHAN: I might need to stay somewhere/

ANNIE: A storm, you reckon/

NATHAN: … for the night.

ANNIE: I don't think they've built a Hilton on the island yet.

NATHAN: Fine, I'll go stay with Uncle Martin.

ANNIE: Fine.

NATHAN: They still might make it.

ANNIE: You should know about them August winds this time of year.

NATHAN: It's October.

ANNIE: Bloody greenhouse fucked up everything.

    Flashback.

FAITH: Annie, tie down those corro sheets on the chook shed. Big storm. Those August winds coming. I can feel it, a proper big storm.

    Back to the present day.

NATHAN: I don't want to be here any longer than I have to.

ANNIE: Nothing new in that.

NATHAN: What is your problem?

ANNIE: (Listen to you.) What is your problem? You ever think it's *your* problem. Smart-arse prick coming in and pushing us around…

NATHAN: When have you ever been around?…

ANNIE: Now it comes out. Come on, let it all out, then. Tell me the shit she fed you. Come on. I know what you're going to say. I'm some kind of whore, some slut who didn't have the sense to love her kids properly. I know what she told you…

NATHAN: Who?

ANNIE: That bitch we buried.

NATHAN: I'm not talking to you…

ANNIE: That's right, off you go/ catch your plane, your fucken water taxi… too busy to talk to your own mother.

NATHAN: My mother?

ANNIE: [*lifting up her top*] I got the scars to prove it, smart arse/ I'm your mother whether you like it or not.

NATHAN: (I'm going to Uncle Martin's.) I'll be back in the morning.

ANNIE: I haven't decided whether I want to give you the table.

NATHAN: What is it worth to you?

ANNIE: It's mine now, isn't it?/ She left it all to me. She didn't leave you anything.

NATHAN: I've never asked you… (for anything before.) [*Pause.*] If you don't want money, what do you want?

ANNIE: Land rights! When do we want it? Now!

> *She laughs.*

NATHAN: I think—It's useless…

ANNIE: I think I'm turning Japanese, I think I'm turning Japanese…

NATHAN: Annie. Shut up!

> *Silence.*

Nana wanted me to have it.

ANNIE: Then why did she leave it to me?

NATHAN: [*yelling*] Just give it to me, Annie. (This is all I have left.)

ANNIE: She was my mother, not yours.

NATHAN: Is that what this is about?

ANNIE: What?

NATHAN: You being/ jealous of me. That Nana …

ANNIE: You're so full of shit.

ANNIE *walks away.*

NATHAN: You get everything, but the one thing I want—(you fight me for), like the table means anything to you—

ANNIE: What the fuck would you know?

NATHAN: Tell me, then. Go on, tell me why you want it…

ANNIE: I don't have to tell you nothing.

NATHAN: No, come on mother, enlighten me.

ANNIE: Bugger off.

NATHAN: Let me be enthralled by your erudite explanations.

ANNIE: Fuck off.

NATHAN: Go on, don't hold back, Annie, dispense me a bit of your wisdom. Pass on some of your vast knowledge.

ANNIE: Don't you speak to me like that.

NATHAN: Give me your theories on the world. Recite us your grand hypothesis.

ANNIE: Fuck off, I said! [*Pause.*] You go on about black this and black that—I'm your elder smart arse/ you want to be black you start showing me some respect. You come here with your big words… thinking to run rings around me with your university bullshit. You can't choose your family. There's a bit of wisdom for you, prick. I'm still your mother whether you like it or not. And she was my mother whether I liked it or not, and I never bad-mouthed my mother to her face like you do. I showed her respect. You know what family is? Do you? Growing up here all sheltered—it's full of secrets/ and lies/ and we all—every one of us/ we'd rather tell those stories from long ago than tell each other the truth from today/ now/ here. You know what family is? It's not blood/ fucken most of the island's got the same blood, but I wouldn't call half them arseholes my family—family is respect. When that's gone, then no use calling yourself black no more. There'll be no blackfellas left when that's gone… You want to feel what it's like having no family/ do ya?/ You walk with me through this place and watch your own blood turn away from you—can't look you in the eye… that's not respect, that's not family. No wonder this place is falling apart [*yelling*] everyone's got their heads so far up their arse they don't know what sunshine is no more!

Silence.

NATHAN: I'm sorry.

ANNIE: Yes you are.

NATHAN: I didn't mean to…

ANNIE: Yes you did.

NATHAN: I had no right to…

ANNIE: No you didn't. [*Pause.*] No matter… a cuppa tea will solve it all. I take mine white with three.

NATHAN: You shouldn't have so much sugar…

ANNIE: What, you reckon I'm sweet enough, eh! Go on.

> NATHAN *exits.*

Hey! Old Girl… you there? Why'd you go off and fucken die for?… I know, I know… Don't go using them words in my house. What've you done to this boy? Here I am, back in this house with nowhere to go… You're a crafty old bitch, you are… You're sly… you're sly.

♦ ♦ ♦ ♦ ♦

SCENE SIX: MEMORY FROM 1969

ANNIE *relives a conversation with* FAITH.

Snap change of mood.

FAITH: Annie, the boy needs his mother.

ANNIE: Well, you be his fucken mother, then.

FAITH: Mind your mouth. [*Pause.*] It ain't our war… You don't even know where Vietnam is.

ANNIE: I don't care.

FAITH: The boy's only three months old…

ANNIE: I'm not hanging around here no more.

FAITH: It's a war, Annie.

ANNIE: And what's this place? This place is hell.

FAITH: But the boy, Annie, the boy…

ANNIE: Suffer the little children

FAITH: Don't… (go using the Lord's words in vain.)

ANNIE: I'm on the next barge and if you don't want to take him then I'll drop 'im off at the church.

FAITH: Why are you doing this to me?

ANNIE: You? Doing this to you?

FAITH: I want you to stay…

ANNIE: So you can look after me?

FAITH: [*crying*] Annie, come on…

ANNIE: You want to look after me?

FAITH: Annie…

ANNIE: Well, you're too late. You're too fucken late…

FAITH: Just come and sit down, just come and talk about it.

ANNIE: No, no, no—Cookie's Table ain't going to solve it. You're not going to pull that one… start talking old stories. You reckon I should forget the past/ well, I am/ all of it. That boy was never born for me, and you/ you were never my mother—and this whole fucken place has nothing to do with me. I'm leaving and this whole fucken island can sink into the ocean and I wouldn't shed a single tear. It could sink into the ocean with you and him on it and not a single drop.

FAITH: If you walk out that door, God help you, you won't be coming back here. Do you hear me, Annie?

ANNIE *exits.*

Annie? Annie? Annie. You'll never be happy if you leave this island. Do you hear me, you'll never be happy.

Blackout.

♦ ♦ ♦ ♦ ♦

SCENE SEVEN

ANNIE: This is the story of Kawana and the great fire.

The story goes something like this… When Cookie hadn't heard from her man she finally accepted he wasn't coming back, she got real shitty—not just everyday shitty, I mean real shitty like she had a fire burning inside of her. She didn't eat for two weeks and her head was churning itself up, stoking that fire so it was white hot. The food she cooked for them people made them sick and when they told her to stop cooking and wash dishes, they still got sick. Like the hate was coming out in the water. And she was burning a fever like you wouldn't believe/ she could put her hands into boiling water and not get scolded, put her hands deep into the ovens without a burn on her. Them old women took Cookie's kids down to the camp to look after them.

The story goes… she called for her boys to be brought up to the house and for her daughter to be taken to another family, like she was being promised. When Cookie greeted them old women at the door they knew something was wrong. Cookie took the two boys and locked the big door from the inside. She took her two sons, sat them on the table in the middle of the kitchen and hugged them close, singing them a song her mother had sung to her.

No one can be certain how the fire started, but the old women say that Cookie had so much hate in her that she just burst into flames.

The white men started a chain of buckets stretching from the well to the front of the house, but the blackfellas were all at the back watching the flames shooting through the kitchen window, all they could hear was her singing in lingo there in the middle of the flames.

Finally the house was gone, nothing. The only thing left was this table standing in the middle of the ashes.

The story goes… that in the night some of the blackfellas from the camp came and took that table. Took it and gave it to Kawana, her daughter. And they were saying, 'This was your mother's birth tree, that's why she left it, why the fire couldn't take it away. It's yours now.' And Kawana, my grandmother, said… 'Let this table be a home for me. Let it be a home for all the lost and the hungry. May all my children and my children's children eat at this table.'

♦ ♦ ♦ ♦ ♦

SCENE EIGHT: THE PRESENT DAY

ANNIE *enters singing. She has a sweet voice.*

ANNIE: Fuck, I'm hungry. I'd eat the balls clear off a concrete cow.

NATHAN: There's food in there.

ANNIE: Imagine the steaks you'd get if the Big Cow was real. Fuck.

NATHAN: You should have eaten at the wake. (There was plenty of food.)

ANNIE: Can you order pizza on this God-forsaken island yet?

NATHAN: It's shut Monday to Thursday.

ANNIE: Fuck.

NATHAN: And they don't deliver.

ANNIE: Jesus.

NATHAN: And they only have four toppings.

ANNIE: A choice of four?

NATHAN: Four toppings: tomato sauce, cheese, ham and tinned pineapple.

ANNIE: This place is a backwater. A fucken backwater. No wonder both of us got out of here.

NATHAN: Don't compare… the… two of us.

ANNIE: We both hate this fucken place, son.

NATHAN: This is my home.

ANNIE: (Don't go getting all oogie-boogie on me, Nat.) You got out of here as soon as you could.

NATHAN: I had my reasons.

ANNIE: And so did I… so don't go getting all righteous on me.

NATHAN: At least I came back regularly.

ANNIE: So did I.

NATHAN: Drunk.

ANNIE: You'd drink too if you had to face her.

NATHAN: I remember when you came back.

ANNIE: See, I told you.

NATHAN: You'd come back when your money ran out or your man ran out. Do you see a theme developing?

ANNIE: Clever dick.

NATHAN: You only came back so you could run away again.

ANNIE: Little boys don't see very much.

NATHAN: I saw enough.

ANNIE: Old Girl kept you away most of the time. Those old bitches…

NATHAN: A little respect.

ANNIE: Why?

NATHAN: 'Cause she's dead.

ANNIE: No way I can disappoint her now, is there?

NATHAN: You never hang around for funerals, do you, Annie?

ANNIE: Shut up!

NATHAN: I mean funerals scare you, don't they? You barely got to your own mother's funeral. For that we should be grateful. How many other funerals didn't you make?

ANNIE: You want to go there?

NATHAN: I must have been in Grade Three or Four.

ANNIE: Shut up.

NATHAN: You with your arm in a sling.

ANNIE: Death frightens me.

NATHAN: 'Nathan get me this', 'Nathan get me that'.

ANNIE: Did you hear what I said?

NATHAN: That's such a good reason to skip the funeral of your own daughter's.

ANNIE: You know Jack shit.

NATHAN: I know Uncle Martin dug the graves. I know that Nana made me carve their names under the table. I know that everyone was there but you.

ANNIE: And did she tell you why? Did she tell you everything?

NATHAN: Some things you don't have to be told, they just fit.

ANNIE: How convenient.

NATHAN: That's your buzz word, isn't it, Annie? Convenient. It wasn't convenient to have kids around, so one way or another you were able to get rid of them.

ANNIE: What did you say?

NATHAN: I didn't mean that.

ANNIE: What did you just accuse me of, prick?

NATHAN: Well, you never had to raise your kids, did you?

ANNIE: You don't know fuck all, shit for brains! What else did she tell you? These fucken stories go round and round and you leave out the bits that don't fit. That's how it works, Nathan. You should know that. Politicians do it all the time. Squeeze in some truth, enough to stop it being a lie, but leave out all the stuff that really matters, the stuff that complicates it, the human shit. And that's the story you keep telling until everyone believes it, and if you want to say something different, if you want to show another side, you become a liar, 'cause everyone knows the truth. Don't they?

It was an accident. He was a good man. We met on the tent circuit, he'd box or play some guitar and I'd sing. His name was Brian, no Ryan. Tall, and that black skin you could just melt for. He was fun. You wouldn't understand, but he could really make the sun shine. He was pissed. I told him to slow down, I told him I should drive, but the cunt just kept going, faster and faster. Normally he'd listen to me—I tried—you got to believe me—I tried. He hit that tree and the girls... You didn't wear seat belts in them days. We were coming back here to pick you up. I bet she didn't tell you that. I thought we could try... try to be a family.

NATHAN: Why didn't you stay?

ANNIE: Her. You know how she got.

NATHAN: They were your daughters.

ANNIE; Okay. I fucked up. Jesus, Nathan, I was twenty-three. (I was a kid.) You never knew her the way I did. You got to believe me.

NATHAN: I couldn't cry for you. I couldn't cry for them.

ANNIE: Well, we all learnt not to cry in this house.

    ANNIE *exits.*

              ◆ ◆ ◆ ◆ ◆

SCENE NINE: MEMORY FROM 1979

NATHAN *remembers a conversation with his grandmother.*

Snap change.

NATHAN *laughs throughout as he watches this memory scene.*

FAITH: [*calling*] Nathan!

YOUNG NATHAN: Yes, Nana.

    FAITH *sets about cleaning* NATHAN *and brushing his hair.*

FAITH: Come on, get ready, young man, spic and span now.

YOUNG NATHAN: I don't want to go.

FAITH: You're going.

YOUNG NATHAN: Naanaaaa.

FAITH: You're going so you better get used to it.

YOUNG NATHAN: Why do we go to church?

FAITH: Because we do.

YOUNG NATHAN: But why?

FAITH: Because God wants us to.

YOUNG NATHAN: But why does he want us to?

FAITH: He wants our souls to be clean.

    Pause.

YOUNG NATHAN: Our souls dirty?

FAITH: Yes, they're dirty.

YOUNG NATHAN: But why do we have to go every week?

FAITH: I told you, to clean our souls.

YOUNG NATHAN: Is my soul that dirty?

FAITH: Yes, your soul is that dirty. Now get yourself ready.

YOUNG NATHAN: If I promised to clean my soul really hard today and not to get it dirty, do I have to go next week?

FAITH: Yes. You have to go every week 'cause a soul like yours can't stay clean.

YOUNG NATHAN: Then why do I bother going at all?

FAITH: Listen here, boy. Your soul's dirty, my soul's dirty, everyone in this flamin' mission has a dirty soul… So don't go thinking you're special. You have to go to church/ So you button that lip and get yourself ready, young man, or you won't be worrying about your dirty soul—

YOUNG NATHAN: /But, Nana, I don't want to go/

FAITH: /If I listened to everything you wanted and didn't want, young man, you would be the mother and I would be the child. Now get!

> FAITH *pushes* YOUNG NATHAN *out, hitting him on the backside with the hairbrush.*
>
> *Blackout.*

◆ ◆ ◆ ◆ ◆

SCENE TEN

FAITH: This is the story of the five virtues, me and my sisters.

The story goes something like this… My mother Kawana worked on the island. She cooked for the mission, for the pastors and their families. They'd rebuilt the house and she'd moved that table straight into the kitchen. She never went far from that table.

She'd been promised to a man from the neighbouring island but he got shipped to a mainland mission and she never got around to looking for him. From all accounts she kept to herself, didn't have much to do with the blacks in the mission. She didn't do the dances or speak the language. There's an old picture of her from the State Museum called 'The Civilised Black' and there she is front row in the centre dressed in white. She must have been forty—I don't know—and she has this really stern face, just how I remember her. Not a hair out of place and every stitch of clothing looks cleaned and pressed within an inch of its life.

People say she had 'lovers'—the sound of boots coming down the verandah to her little room behind the kitchen...

They say her first baby stayed with her until she was four. She named her Hope. And then Hope was taken. And then Joy, and Charity, and then Perseverance, and then me, the youngest... Faith. One by one, each taken away. She kept me the longest. I left when I was six. I was the last, I think.

♦ ♦ ♦ ♦ ♦

SCENE ELEVEN: PRESENT DAY

ANNIE *attempts to grab* FAITH.

NATHAN *carries two cups of tea.*

NATHAN: Mum... Mum/ Annie...

> ANNIE *turns around.*

Where were you?

ANNIE: Nowhere.

NATHAN: No. You were off with the fairies.

ANNIE: Just thinking about your grandmother.

> NATHAN *gives* ANNIE *a cup of tea.*

NATHAN: What?

ANNIE: Nothing—just remembering—I was born here/ on this table. You were born in a hospital, you—me, I was born right here.

NATHAN: I haven't heard that one.

ANNIE: There's lots you don't know, boy.

NATHAN: I'm thirty-five. Think you can stop calling me boy.

ANNIE: Just 'cause you got hair on your balls don't make you a man.

NATHAN: Don't talk (like that)

ANNIE: Don't get hairy with me/

NATHAN: I just don't want to be called/

ANNIE: Get over it.

NATHAN: Annie!—You ever thought how hard it is growing up in this family?

ANNIE: Yes, son, I've lived it.

NATHAN: No, as a male, as a man—no one talks about the men in this family.

ANNIE: Well, maybe 'cause they were all scum.

NATHAN: All of them?

ANNIE: You're better off without them.

NATHAN: Uncle Martin's the closest man…

ANNIE: Yeah, and look at him…

NATHAN: What's wrong with Uncle… (Martin?)

ANNIE: You think I'm a hard head, you should pull your head outta your arse and look at the man properly…

NATHAN: What?

ANNIE: All he does is putt around in the boat of his, fucken telling everyone what the 'old people' did—like he'd know! He's a fucken poser, that's what he is. Little Marty used to wet himself in church, I can tell you now…

NATHAN: So a kid wets himself, that doesn't make him… (weird.)

ANNIE: He was sixteen. He's always been a bit womba, that boy.

NATHAN: He's a man.

ANNIE: [*sexy*] Well, he's never been a man to me…

NATHAN: Oh, Jesus Christ, he's your cousin.

ANNIE: Language, if the Old Girl heard you she'd be fucken rolling in her grave.

> *The sound of thunder rolling.*

There. She'll be coming after you. [*Teasing him*] You'll be burning in hell, my boy, burning with the devil. Eternal damnation.

NATHAN: Piss off.

ANNIE: Now I'm sure you weren't brought up to say them words. Old Girl would have dragged you up proper.

NATHAN: I'm just saying it was hard growing up without men around… as role models. There are no men in this family let alone on this island.

ANNIE: What? You want a bunch of drunks and wife beaters to show you how to be a man? You're better off not knowing them cunts…

NATHAN: Annie …

ANNIE: That's the only way to explain 'em/ cunts/ right and right-out cunts.

The sound of thunder.

They both smile at each other.

NATHAN: Where did they go?

ANNIE: Most of them pissed off the island the first chance they got. The mine used to give 'em jobs, but the government made that law that said they had to get paid the same as white people—'bye-bye jobs—and when the mine closed down, nothing left.

NATHAN: Did they go to the mainland?

ANNIE: No, most of them down that hill with your grandmother. There were never any good men on this island. Billy Boy drank most of his waking hours so when he didn't wake up no one thought anything of it. Heart. Fucken pickled his balls before he had the chance to do anything with them. Jimmy drowned himself—stupid bastard—you grow up on an island and you don't learn how to swim. Fucken serves him right. Then Pete pissed off long ago/ good on him, got away from that prick of a father. There you go, Uncle Stevie Salter, a cunt of the highest order. Now why would you want him around to fuck your life up?

NATHAN: Where did he go?

ANNIE: Carked it in the seventies. Strung himself up under the house. There's no men here 'cause they either pissed off or died, son, that's the truth. We're here for a good time, not a long time.

NATHAN: It would have been good to have…

ANNIE: Well, when you have a family of your own you can stick around and be the good fucken father figure.

NATHAN: What was he like?

ANNIE: You married?

NATHAN: No. Was he good-looking?

ANNIE: You got kids… well, any you know of?

NATHAN: [*definitely*] No.

ANNIE: You sure?

NATHAN: Certain.

ANNIE: What, you got no dick?

NATHAN: We were talking about my father.

ANNIE: You had a dick when you were born.

NATHAN: Annie.

ANNIE: If you've gone and lost it. Well, that's your fault.

NATHAN: I'm not going to have kids.
ANNIE: What, your career too important?
NATHAN: No.
ANNIE: What, you hate kids, or something?
NATHAN: No.

    Silence.

ANNIE: Fuck me senseless. You're a poof!
NATHAN: I could still have kids.
ANNIE: I knew it. My son's a fucken fag. Did she know?
NATHAN: We never talked about it.
ANNIE: Fucken hell.
NATHAN: You really don't know me.
ANNIE: My son's a queero. Fucken… fuck.
NATHAN: Could you stop that?

    Pause.

ANNIE: Well, you didn't get it from me.
NATHAN: I haven't got a disease.
ANNIE: You wear one of them things?…
NATHAN: What?
ANNIE: [*coyly*] A French letter… you got to wear them things, Nathan…
NATHAN: Okay, I heard you!

    Pause.

ANNIE: You ever done it with a woman?
NATHAN: Once or twice.
ANNIE: Then you're half-and-half.
NATHAN: No.
ANNIE: You might grow out of it.
NATHAN: I might, but it's unlikely.
ANNIE: Maybe you should try harder.
NATHAN: I knew I shouldn't have told you.
ANNIE: I blame that university, she should never have sent you away.
NATHAN: Don't bring Nana into this.
ANNIE: If you'd stayed on the island this wouldn't have happened. Fucken universities with all that free thinking and shit… No one touched you, did they? Here… no one messed with ya? You tell me which ones and I'll go bust 'em right now.

NATHAN: Can we forget this conversation?

Silence.

ANNIE: Which one are you? Top or bottom?

ANNIE *does hand gestures to explain.*

NATHAN: I'm not answering that.

ANNIE: It hurts, doesn't it? I mean, you got to get all loose first...

NATHAN: Annie, I am not swapping notes on sex!

ANNIE: Go on, you can tell (me).

NATHAN: Annie!

Pause.

ANNIE: Shit. Then you really aren't going to have kids, are you?

NATHAN: Well, not by accident.

ANNIE: Tell you what, though, if you ever do... I think I'd be a 'Granny',
no, maybe 'Grandma'.

NATHAN: Maybe you'd just be Annie.

ANNIE: No fucken way, I let you get away with it but little ones will
have to do it properly.

NATHAN: Who said you'd have anything to do with them?

ANNIE: You wouldn't stop me from seeing...

NATHAN: It doesn't matter.

ANNIE: Yes it does. I want to be a 'Granny'. That's the next step. That's
why you have kids.

NATHAN: I'm sorry to let you down.

ANNIE: Never too late to change. God works in mysterious ways.

NATHAN: Not that mysterious.

ANNIE: They're the thing that makes you understand death, you know.

NATHAN: Annie... (get off my case.)

ANNIE: Think of it like this, see—like the beach/ sand gets washed out
to sea and new sand gets washed in—someone pops off one end and
someone is born, see?

NATHAN: Very zen.

ANNIE *smiles at* NATHAN.

The sound of thunder rolls in. The storm is getting closer.

ANNIE: That storm's coming.

NATHAN *pulls out his phone. He dials.*

That water taxi'll be moored up for the night and that last barge must have gone by now. Reckon you'll just have to stay here, then.

NATHAN: [*into the phone*] Uncle Martin?… Just tell him I'm coming down… It's Nat… Okay, 'bye-bye.

ANNIE: You going?

NATHAN: (Yep.)

Pause. Thunder.

ANNIE: But it's going to piss down.

NATHAN: I better go now.

Pause.

ANNIE: Son…

NATHAN: Do you want me to?…

ANNIE: You don't need to… (go.)

NATHAN: You need me to stay or not?

ANNIE: I don't need you.

NATHAN: You'll be right, then?

ANNIE: I'm hairy enough to look after myself. Don't need no help from no one.

NATHAN: Okay.

Pause.

ANNIE: There'll be a houseful down there.

NATHAN: There'll be room for one more.

ANNIE: Go on, plenty of beds here.

NATHAN: I better go…

ANNIE: Don't leave in the storm, son.

NATHAN: Mum…

ANNIE: Fuck you, then. Piss off.

NATHAN: Nice.

ANNIE: Fuck off, faggot.

NATHAN: I'll see you in the morning.

ANNIE: Yeah.

NATHAN: I'll be back before the first barge to pick up the table.

NATHAN *exits.*

ANNIE: [*yelling*] In your dreams, mister… fucken in your dreams.

♦ ♦ ♦ ♦ ♦

SCENE TWELVE: 1964 AND PRESENT DAY

A huge thunder clap and rain starts to fall.

The memory of FAITH *becomes real for* ANNIE.

ANNIE: Jesus!

FAITH: Mind your language in this house, young lady.

ANNIE: Mum?

FAITH: No need to take his name in vain.

ANNIE: Sorry, Mum.

FAITH: It's only a storm. Good sign, storms. Summer's coming.

ANNIE: What are you doing here?

FAITH: It's only the angels moving God's furniture around.

ANNIE: You aren't here.

FAITH: Come here, Annie. I'll let you comb my hair.

ANNIE: But storms always scare me.

FAITH: Why now?

ANNIE: 'Cause they remind me... the Hairy Man.

FAITH: Who told you that rubbish?

ANNIE: Uncle Stevie said the Hairy Man hides in the storms.

FAITH: Don't you go listening to him. I'll look after that Hairy Man if he comes looking for my Annie.

   Lighting and thunder.

It's a good sign. The storm's saying that summer is on the way. It'll give everything a good cleanout.

ANNIE: I'm frightened.

FAITH: Why, now?

ANNIE: 'Cause they remind me...

FAITH: If you ever get frightened, you just say that Lord's Prayer now... come on... hands in the proper way... Our Father...

FAITH & ANNIE: [*together*] Our Father, who art in Heaven, hallowed be Thy name. Thy Kingdom come, Thine will be done on Earth as it is in Heaven. Give us this day our daily bread and forgive us our trespasses as we forgive those who trespass against us. Lead us not unto temptation... (and deliver us from evil, for Thine is the Kingdom, the power, and the glory, for ever and ever. Amen.)

ANNIE: [*overlapping the end of the prayer*] 'Cause they remind me...
You never believed me. I was some slut/ some whore who turned her
back on God. You were gone to a church meeting on the mainland.
I kicked up such a stink, you said you'd pray for my soul. And it
rained and the lightning/ like the sky was ripping apart, like a war
was happening. Like the devil himself was being cast out of heaven.
And he was—he came in the shape of a man soaked, in black, and he
held me down and I said that prayer—Our father who art in heaven/
He took off his wet clothes, he said they needed to dry—He told
me I was pretty. No one had called me pretty before. And then he
grabbed my arm and pulled me close to him/ He held me against his
wet black skin and he smelt... of stale piss and cigarettes. He told
me I was pretty and he kissed me on my bare neck, he grabbed my
hair and he touched me. My own uncle... I was thirteen. He called
me pretty and then he called me a slut. He took my innocence. They
must have heard me scream, they must have heard me call out but
no one came—no one came to help.

> *A crack of thunder and the lights of the house go out.*

> ANNIE *and* FAITH *are dimly lit.*

I was thirteen. You were meant to look after me. You were meant
to believe me. I have not got a dirty soul... I have not got a dirty
soul... You were meant to believe me... believe me. Do you hear
me? If you walk out that door... 'Set the table, Annie. I'm cooking
a big feed.' 'Set the table Annie.' 'Sylvia Anne, set the table.' I'll
fucken set the table, you bitch. I'll fucken set it for you...

> ANNIE *is going mad. She smashes plates instead of setting the
> table.*

> *A figure enters, silhouetted. He is wet and black, in a coat. He
> carries a hurricane lamp.*

> *The figure is* NATHAN. *He rushes forward trying to stop* ANNIE.
> *She struggles against him, hitting him.*

> *The storm is wild outside.*

> ANNIE *pushes the table over and underneath it the family tree is
> illuminated—a magical carving of names in an ornate pattern.*

NATHAN: Annie, it's Nathan. It's all right.

Blackout.

A huge crack of thunder.

Silence.

END OF ACT ONE

ACT TWO

SCENE ONE

ANNIE: This is the story of Faith and the house.

The story goes something like this... Faithie married a man like she'd choose a hat and gloves—easy, reliable and not too uncomfortable. She was cooking for a cattle station and doing the droves. Anyway, no sooner had she got pregnant than the fool fell off his horse and broke his neck. So there she was, a widow, black and pregnant. Now the story goes that this fella was good with his cash, seems he used to be a serious gambler, behind Faithie's back. So when he died she got big heaps of money/ six thousand or sixty thousand or a million/ who cares, a heap anyway. So Faith gets it into her head to get back to the island. So she packs up her shit— pregnant, mind/ she packs up her shit and then she heads off. Belly popping out, stopping off in towns, getting a bit of work, getting a letter from the local pastor or bullyman to get to the next little town and so on and so. If you believed her stories, she fucken built the road and pulled the fucken dray herself. Anyway, she gets back here and walks straight into this house, the house she remembers—and— it's empty/ fucken cobwebs everywhere. It's empty. Like it's been waiting for her. And in the kitchen is that table—Cookie's Table.

Well, she walks down to the mission house, throws that money across at some stupid white cunt and says, 'I'm buying that house.'

Don't worry, this family tree business gets complicated. Cookie had her daughter Kawana, who had five daughters which Faith was the youngest, who had me. It's easy enough to remember 'cause it's all carved on the bottom of the table. Like, some people put it in the front of their Bible, it's all under here—all the blood family back to Cookie... well, all the family we know.

♦ ♦ ♦ ♦ ♦

SCENE TWO: PRESENT DAY

NATHAN *appears in his designer underwear. He has a waxed chest and a gym-sculpted body. He carries the delivered morning paper wrapped in plastic. He goes into the kitchen and returns with a bottle of milk. He drinks.*

ANNIE *appears dressed in a nightie which has 'World's Best Mum' printed on it.* NATHAN *is startled. He's embarrassed.*

ANNIE: Nothing I haven't seen before.

NATHAN: You snuck up on me.

ANNIE: I don't sneak in my own house.

NATHAN: Nana used to whistle in the morning.

ANNIE: Well, I ain't her.

NATHAN: I'm going to get decent.

ANNIE: I'm your mother, for Christ's sake.

> *Silence.*

Sit down.

> NATHAN *reluctantly sits back down and continues drinking the milk.*

Is there enough for my tea?

> NATHAN *puts the bottle down and pushes it towards her.*

Errrr… backwash.

NATHAN: I'll go get some more.

ANNIE: Don't worry, what's a bit of spit between family? You want breakfast? I'll cook us up some eggs—and stuff.

NATHAN: No. (I'll be right.)

> ANNIE *gets up and goes into the kitchen. She puts on the electric kettle.*

ANNIE: That fucken wood stove.

NATHAN: What's wrong with it?

ANNIE: Fuck me. I can't believe she still used the bugger? Fucken martyr. She could do it every time/ even from the fucken grave she can still make me feel guilty.

NATHAN: Can we just start the day without that word?
ANNIE: Fuck breakfast, then.

> *Silence.*

You're not a bad-looking lad. But you lot always look after yourself?
NATHAN: Thanks. (Not!)
ANNIE: You filled out nicely.

> *She gives him the thumbs up.*

> *Silence.*

How did you go in the downstairs department.
NATHAN: Sorry?
ANNIE: [*indicating size*] How's the boodu?
NATHAN: Annie!
ANNIE: I'm your mother, I should know these things.
NATHAN: You missed that chance.

> *Silence.*

ANNIE: Why haven't you got any hair on your body, boy?
NATHAN: I'm getting dressed.
ANNIE: Even I got hair on my chest.

> ANNIE *tries to get a closer look.* NATHAN *exits.*

> ANNIE *laughs herself silly.*

You want to be a man, but you still want to be a boy. [*Laughing*] Did you hear me? I said, you want to…
NATHAN: [*offstage*] I heard you.

> ANNIE *picks up the milk bottle and rubs at the ring it's left on the table. Taking a tea towel from the kitchen door she cleans the spot.*

ANNIE: I met plenty of your kind, you know. I was an entertainer, I was. Heaps of fags in that business. They'd wax their chests, too. Steal your best make-up, some of them. But nice 'girls'. Always good for a laugh, quick with a yarn… I pissed myself so often with them mob. But cruel unhappy they was. Good fighters. Had to be. Sometimes there'd be bruises from here to their arsehole, true. I wonder what happened to them now. Most probably dead, poor things. Black and white ones. See, you ain't alone. Maybe you take after me—you could have been an entertainer.

NATHAN *re-enters dressed in his suit.*

NATHAN: I don't do drag. Never have. I think it's degrading for women.

ANNIE: No good you getting all serious on me now.

NATHAN: [*referring to the paper*] I'll cancel the paper on my way to the barge… Unless you want it delivered.

ANNIE: [*teasing* NATHAN] I don't know, might go away for a bit.

NATHAN: What about the house?

ANNIE: Rent it out. You'd get a good rent this close to the beach, I reckon. Some tourist'd take it. Rough it for a bit with that stove/ Fuck it! Why didn't the woman get a 'lectric one?

> NATHAN's *phone rings. His dialogue is in the background.* ANNIE *talks over the top of him.*

I can just see her now, hauling wood in from the shed. Bitch… and she'd do it just to spite me, too…

NATHAN: [*into the phone*] Hello… Yeah thanks, Peter… No I got caught in the storm—tell him thanks from my family/ and say I said thanks for the flowers.

ANNIE: You know who I hated?… That little match girl in that story— sitting in the snow selling matches/ stupid bitch—sitting there feeling sorry for herself. Just like the Old Girl—all she had to do is—well, do something…

NATHAN: [*into the phone*] Mr Mori rang about the contract and I said I'd get onto that first thing today…

ANNIE: Stupid little match girl/ All she had to do was set fire to the house and she wouldn't have fucken froze to death—looking through the flamin' window dreaming about being inside dancing or whatever the Christ they were doing in there.

NATHAN: [*into the phone*] Yes I know the Minister has a meeting—I can meet him there/ it's only forty-five minutes by water taxi to the city…

ANNIE: Is that the Prime Minister?

NATHAN: [*to* ANNIE] Quiet!— [*Into the phone*] I have some business here to sort out first…

ANNIE: Tell him we want land rights, 'lectric stove and he can shove his apology up his arse.

NATHAN: [*to* ANNIE] *Shut up!*

ANNIE: Though he might like it up the arse, too.

NATHAN: [*to* ANNIE] Annie.

ANNIE: Give him here, I'll sort him out.

NATHAN: [*into the phone*] I'll ring when I'm on my way. [*He hangs up.*] Thank you very much.

ANNIE: Was that him? Was that the old cranky bastard?

NATHAN: I have to be gone by one.

ANNIE: You just buried your grandmother, surely they can wait another day or so.

NATHAN: They need me.

ANNIE: You're a hard boy, Nathan Yeoman.

NATHAN: I just deal with things differently.

> *Pause.*

ANNIE: You got someone… you know, someone special?

NATHAN: There was someone.

ANNIE: What happened? Did he die?

NATHAN: Not every gay man dies. It just didn't work out.

ANNIE: I loved a man once/ actually I loved several men—some of them all at the same time/ did you tell her about this fella?

NATHAN: No, never got around to it.

ANNIE: How long was you with him?

NATHAN: Nine years.

ANNIE: Nine years? And you never got around to it?

NATHAN: It never came up.

ANNIE: But you told me.

NATHAN: I didn't tell you…

ANNIE: You told me and you never told her.

NATHAN: It never came up…

ANNIE: [*smiling to herself*] Well, I'm gonna go and get decent, too. Can't sit around all day flashing my muppi, can I now?

> ANNIE *exits. As she leaves, she touches* NATHAN's *shoulder.*

Happy birthday, son.

> NATHAN *remembers something and blindly digs around under the table with his hand, eventually finding a postcard.*

♦ ♦ ♦ ♦ ♦

SCENE THREE: MEMORY OF 1979

NATHAN *has memory of his tenth birthday.*

FAITH *and* YOUNG NATHAN *sit at the table. In front of* YOUNG NATHAN *is a half-eaten birthday cake with candles. He stares at the cake.*

ANNIE *enters. She's been drinking. She sings and re-lights the candles on the cake.*

ANNIE: [*singing*]
>Happy birthday to you,
>Happy birthday to you,
>Happy birthday, Mr President,
>Happy birthday to you.

>*She claps.*

I got you a present—somewhere …

>*She rummages in her handbag and eventually puts an ashtray in front of* YOUNG NATHAN.

Sorry didn't get time to wrap it. Happy birthday, son. I'm starving…

FAITH: We've eaten.

YOUNG NATHAN: She can have some cake.

FAITH: We've had our dinner, an hour ago.

ANNIE: Be a love, Nathan, and cut me a piece. [*To* FAITH] I'm here *now*.

FAITH: Where've you been?/ The barge got in at four.

ANNIE: I was delayed.

FAITH: He got all excited, said we had to be down there early and that barge came in—not there, so we waited for the five-thirty, thinking she must have missed it, but no sight of you.

ANNIE: I was tied up I said.

>YOUNG NATHAN *hands her a piece of cake.*

[*Getting the giggles*] Is that the suit?

FAITH: [*to* YOUNG NATHAN] I told you it was too small.

YOUNG NATHAN: You can take me dancing now.

FAITH: You sent him a suit that was too small.

ANNIE: [*with a laugh*] Dancing?

YOUNG NATHAN: Like how you said…

He gives her the postcard. She reads it.

You said you'd take me dancing.

ANNIE: Did I?

YOUNG NATHAN: I packed my port.

FAITH: Tell him straight, Annie. Tell him you can't take him with you/ tell him now.

ANNIE: Where did I say I was going to take you dancing?

NATHAN: Top of the Town, there on the postcard.

FAITH: Tell him now, how he's been wasting his time.

ANNIE: You and me dancing at the Top of the Town. We'd have to get you a better suit… My little man and me.

FAITH: Don't toy with him.

ANNIE: I'm not talking to you. [*To* YOUNG NATHAN] How rude… (your Nana is.)

YOUNG NATHAN: I can go with you.

FAITH: Annie!

YOUNG NATHAN: I've got my port.

ANNIE: We can go dancing—Top of the Town you say.

YOUNG NATHAN: Yes.

ANNIE: You and me can do that.

FAITH: You aren't taking him away.

ANNIE: He's my son.

ANNIE *takes a drink from a bottle of Jack Daniels.*

YOUNG NATHAN: Mum.

ANNIE *doesn't respond.*

Mum.

ANNIE: Oh, me… yes, love.

YOUNG NATHAN: When are we going?

ANNIE: Let's go now. Right now.

FAITH: He's not going.

ANNIE: Got your port packed then, have you?

YOUNG NATHAN *nods.*

Well, go on. Go grab it and we'll be off to dance away the night at the Top of the Town.

YOUNG NATHAN *stands and watches from the side of stage.*

ANNIE *eats her cake.*

You got some of this to take on the road. I want to have the cake and eat it, too.

She laughs.

FAITH: You stupid girl.

ANNIE: I'm twenty-five—I'm a woman.

FAITH: You're not taking the boy. Did you hear me? You're not going to take him.

ANNIE: You said that already.

FAITH: You're not going to take him. You are not going to take him. You are not taking him away from me.

ANNIE: Away from *you*… oooohhhh!

FAITH: You are not going to take him from this house.

ANNIE: Well, we'll let Natty decide that, shall we?

FAITH: You never wanted the boy.

ANNIE: Well, I've changed my mind. He's my son.

FAITH: Yes, a son you was going to leave on the steps of the church.

ANNIE: Well, I've changed.

FAITH: No you haven't.

ANNIE: I've grown up.

FAITH: I knew this was a mistake…

ANNIE: What?

FAITH: Letting you back in.

ANNIE: [*thumping her chest*] I'm his mother.

FAITH: You're not ready to be a mother. You haven't earned it. You haven't earnt the right to be a mother.

ANNIE: And you have?!

FAITH: God will be my judge.

ANNIE: Then let God sit in judgement of me, too.

FAITH: The boy belongs here.

ANNIE: I'll be doing him a favour.

FAITH: This is his home.

ANNIE: Home, my arse.

FAITH: Here…

ANNIE: It's a hole.

FAITH: You can ruin your life all you like, that's between you and God/ I will not sit back and watch you ruin the boy's life.

ANNIE: I'm his mother, for fuck's sake.

FAITH: What kind of mother are you going to be? A drunk, a loose woman, never settling in one place, never putting a meal on the table, never holding down a decent job/ You, rushing to your grave.

ANNIE: [*crying, she knows the truth*] That's going to change.

FAITH: And the men…

ANNIE: No.

FAITH: All the men. And what are you going to do with the boy then? What are you going to do when you're passed out on the floor—and some man comes—and mucks around with your boy. How are you going to look after him then… huh… what are you going to do flaked out drunk in some gutter… how are you going to look after him?

ANNIE *is visibly shaken.*

ANNIE: [*crying*] Fuck off.

FAITH: You have to be careful, you have to keep an eye out…

ANNIE: Fuck you… Fuck you…

FAITH: You don't want what happened to you… for the good of the boy.

ANNIE: [*crying*] I want to come home, Mumu. Let me back. I'm sorry. I don't want to go again… please, Mum, I'll be good, I promise. I want to come home…

ANNIE *holds out her arms as if needing* FAITH *to hug her.* FAITH *is stone.* ANNIE *picks up her bag and walks out. She turns to see* YOUNG NATHAN *step forward carrying his port, stuffed full. She exits.*

YOUNG NATHAN: Mum? Mummy! Where're you going?

FAITH *holds the boy close.*

Where's she going?

FAITH: She's gone now.

YOUNG NATHAN: When's she coming back?

FAITH: She's not, love. She's gone now for good. Don't worry. We can get back to normal now.

YOUNG NATHAN: I want to go with her.

FAITH: She had to go alone.

YOUNG NATHAN: You made her go away.

FAITH: She had to go.

YOUNG NATHAN: You made her go. I hate you! I hate you.

YOUNG NATHAN *runs off back to his room.*

FAITH *clears the cake and plates and exits.*

◆ ◆ ◆ ◆ ◆

SCENE FOUR: PRESENT DAY

NATHAN *is under the table looking up. He's carving a name.* ANNIE *enters, carrying some papers.*

ANNIE: What are you doing?

NATHAN: Carving his name.

ANNIE: Who?

NATHAN: Ryan... whoever he is.

ANNIE: Harris.

NATHAN: Thank you. Ryan Harris.

ANNIE: What are you doing that for?

NATHAN: The girls deserve a father.

ANNIE: Fuck, Nathan. What do you have to go do that for? Jesus. (That was so long ago.)

NATHAN: Too many gaps.

ANNIE: Jesus, son. He didn't mean anything... He didn't deserve to be put... there/ there.

NATHAN: A few men on here wouldn't go astray.

ANNIE: But that's for family... proper family

NATHAN: God works in mysterious ways.

ANNIE: Oh, God!

NATHAN: There we go, another member of the family.

ANNIE: That's vandalism, that is.

NATHAN: That's what the table's for... family. Those that make it and those that don't.

ANNIE: Ryan Harris. Jesus.

NATHAN: Cookie, Kawana, Faith, you and me. That's the line. Of course she thought I'd be putting my kids' names here.

ANNIE: But instead you're putting the names of stray men. Your best work must be over the toilet doors of Australia.

NATHAN: What's my father's name?

Silence.

ANNIE *sits down and continues reading the papers.*

Nana made me grow my hair really long. She liked combing it. Everyone thought I was a little girl.

ANNIE: Well, they were right about that.

NATHAN: I never fought it. Never even thought about it. I didn't know what a man really was. I just went along my way, did well at school, did well at uni, got a job, did well at that. It didn't hit me. I just didn't think about it. It didn't worry me. I wanted to ask you who my...

ANNIE: [*referring to the papers*] Did you write this stuff?... It's a load of bullshit.

NATHAN: I really... really... got to go, Annie.

ANNIE: Don't go yet... I'll fire up that fucker and cook us lunch.

NATHAN: I gotta get to the mainland.

ANNIE: We haven't had that blue about the table yet, stay and yarn. Just you and me. And Jack.

ANNIE *pulls out a bottle of Jack Daniels.*

NATHAN: It's a bit early...

ANNIE: Never too early... and never too late to start...

ANNIE *exits.*

[*Offstage*] What you want to write all that stuff about blackfellas for?... I never needed no handouts... lazy bastards get what they deserve.

ANNIE *re-enters with two vegemite glasses. She seems to be getting drunk without drinking.*

NATHAN: You can't say that.

ANNIE: If you ask me, and I don't care you're not asking, no one owes you nothing... you make your own way in this world... best you don't need anyone or anything... You come into this world alone and that's the way you go out, so you better get used to it. You eat, you shit, you eat some more, you shit some more and along the way you fuck a bit... and then you die.

NATHAN: I've seen the t-shirt. How long have you been drinking? (This morning.)

ANNIE: Since before you were born. You see my philosssssophy—is simple. You ready for this?—Don't need anyone. I mean it/ Don't *need* anyone! Not a soul. That's how to live your life and not get hurt.

> *She rolls up her sleeves to reveal attempted suicide scars. She's pouring the drink clumsily.* NATHAN *cleans the table.*

You needed her. That's what your problem is… you needed her too much. You can't see your life without her… I'm right, aren't I?… You need her… Well, she's dead… she's gone and she's not coming back and she's taking all that shit with her to the grave… she's taken all of it… it ain't coming back… she ain't coming back… stupid bitch… You hear me?… You ain't coming back…

> ANNIE *begins to sing a traditional song.*

NATHAN: Annie!

ANNIE: I'm your mother… you call me mother… fuck ya… you start to pay me some respect… I brought you into this world and I can take you out…

NATHAN: Annie, calm down… (sit down.)

ANNIE: Don't tell me what to do… I'm the mother here… do you hear me?… I'm the mother here… If I listened to what you wanted all the time then you'd be the mother, but you're not… I'm the fucken mother…

NATHAN: You… (were never my mother.)

ANNIE: I'm the fucken mother. I gave birth to you. I went through all that fucking pain. I'm the mother. What did she go through? What did she ever do? Fuck all. That's what. Fuck all.

> NATHAN's *phone rings. He goes to exit.* ANNIE *takes a drink.* NATHAN *switches his phone to message bank. Silence. Break of mood.*

NATHAN: I almost drowned once. Nana took me out to the end of the jetty and threw me in. Said it was the way she learnt to swim. Must have been around the time Jimmy drowned. I must have been six… before school, anyway. She just picked me up and hurled me into the sea. There I am coughing and spluttering, bobbing up and down, arms everywhere, taking a breath and sinking down. Pushing up again and then sinking. I remember hearing Nana yelling. Hearing half of everything she said. Next thing you know, there's this huge splash and Nana's in there, clothes and all. [*With a laugh*] She used to make me grow my hair really long, she used to brush it a lot. She grabs me by the hair and she lifts me above the water. She's holding me up out of the water by my hair and she's under the water. The water's deep... high tide, and she's holding me up. I couldn't see her face... She's holding me out of the water and I'm crying and coughing up half the ocean and she's moving closer to the jetty. She didn't take a breath, she just moved closer to the jetty. She stayed under the water the whole time. When she got out, she was real pale, I remember... and she gave me the biggest flogging. True. I'd forgotten that.

    Pause.

ANNIE: Lucky you.

    Pause.

NATHAN: I want you to stay away from me, this is not going to work... I don't want you ringing me, or asking for money or anything... Just give me what I want.

    ANNIE *is tapping the table.*

Why do you want it?

ANNIE: It's mine. Why do *you* want it?

NATHAN: It's my history...

ANNIE: You got those stories...

NATHAN: It's not the same...

ANNIE: No...

NATHAN: You haven't been back here in years.

ANNIE: Well, I'm back now and that shits you.

    Silence.

This table tells me I come from somewhere, when I'm in another fucked-up mess, in another city with some deadshit, or on the road again, on the run again...

    She attempts to sing 'On the Road Again'.

I dream about it, that's what I'm saying—I dream about it. I have memories of sitting here/ and I can feel it/ like all the people who came before me are sitting here, cooking or eating or reading or— [*Smiling*]

The talk and the years… You don't have the fucken monopoly on feelings. All the good times and the worst times I ever had were around this table.

A kookaburra is heard in the distance.

You don't know me… you don't know me or what I've done. [*Pause.*] I have stories for every part of this country/ I could tell you shit that would curl your hair. This whole place is held together with stories and songs, and lies and things best left unsaid—you want to remember/ well, I want to forget—you spin silk out of shit…

What are you going to do with it? Give it pride of place like some trophy/ you don't have family, you've turned your back on us/ that's right/ you pointing the stinky finger, but you the one now—I did my bit—I had kids. You/ you got no one to pass stuff on to—what's the fucken use of knowing them stories when all you're going to do is take 'em to the grave? Years and years/ time ends with you/ no one/ that's who's getting this table after us. You call me selfish—'my career'…

NATHAN: She wanted me to have a career…

ANNIE: Well, where were you when she died? Where were you?

She lights a cigarette.

Silence.

Look at us—the fag and the spinster… arguing over/ neither of us going to have anyone to pass on to/ neither of us is going to have anyone to give anything to… we, both of us will pass on fuck all.

The sound of women singing a church song in the distance.

ANNIE *joins in. She has a good voice.*

Hey, I heard this joke… What do you call a Murri with a Mercedes?… A thief. What do you call a bunch of Land Council Murris busting for a piss?… A tribe-urinal. What do you call a Murri fella with a gun? You call that fella anything he wants.

NATHAN: Tribe-urinal… I haven't heard that one.

ANNIE: Good, eh! Made that one up. 'Cause you piss in a urinal and they're a tribe, see…

NATHAN: Yeah… I got it.

ANNIE: You got any jokes?

NATHAN: Nah.

ANNIE: Come on, I reckon you could be real funny.

NATHAN: No. Not noted for being funny.

ANNIE: Well, you try out one of them jokes, then.

NATHAN: Yeah, I will.

Pause.

ANNIE: No, now. Tell that urinal one.

NATHAN: You just told it. (It won't be funny now.)

ANNIE: I'll gamin pretend that it's the first time I'm hearing it.

NATHAN: It won't be funny, Annie!

ANNIE: Try it… go on.

NATHAN: This is ridiculous… No. You just said that joke a minute ago. You can't go repeating the same thing straight away. It won't be funny.

ANNIE: Who said?

NATHAN: No one said. It just is.

ANNIE: I reckon there's been a gap in your upbringing, my lad. Who ever heard of a Murri who couldn't tell a yarn?

NATHAN: I'm just saying it won't be funny. [*Laughing*] We both know it. We both know the joke, so it can't be funny anymore.

ANNIE: Bullshit. [*Smiling*] You tell that joke once and it's funny and then, yeah, maybe you tell that joke again it's not so funny, but if you keep telling that joke it gets funny again. That's how it works.

NATHAN: I don't know about that.

ANNIE: Here, now. What do you call a bunch of Land Council fellas busting for a piss? A *tribe-urinal*. What do you call a big mob of Land Council fellas who can't make up there mind whether they need take a shit or a piss? A *tribe-urinal*. Did you hear that one about those Native Title fellas all lining up holding their boodus, who bust into the High Court and piss all over the judge, and the judge says, 'Hey hey, this is no *tribe-urinal*'.

NATHAN: That's not right. You changed the joke.

ANNIE: No I didn't. It's the same joke. *Tribe-urinal*.

NATHAN: You changed the words…

ANNIE: Yeah, had to… couldn't go repeating the same thing one after the other.

NATHAN: That's what I was saying.

ANNIE: It was the same joke/ same, same, same, just all—different. That's Murri way. Got to find the way of saying the same thing over and over so you can learn it. That's how you pass things on.

NATHAN: Yeah. I never thought about it.

ANNIE: All right, you have a go.

NATHAN: What?

ANNIE: Tell that joke.

> NATHAN *hesitates.* ANNIE *'s hopeful.*

All right, here we go. We'll flip on it. Heads, you have to tell the joke, and tails, you don't. You got a dollar?

NATHAN: [*thinking*] Okay. But I'll toss.

ANNIE: [*doing a rude gesture*] I'm sure you're the best at tossing.

> NATHAN *laughs and tosses the coin. It's heads.*

NATHAN: Okay, okay… got to psych myself into this. A group of Aborigines walk into a—no bust into a courtroom all desperate for the toilet and the judge says, 'I'm sorry but the tribe-urinal is down the hall.'

> ANNIE *gamin laughs her head off, too much.*

I wasn't funny.

ANNIE: Yes you were, son. You were really funny. But no, not really. You need to drink.

NATHAN: I can't drink.

ANNIE: What do you mean can't drink. It's easy.

> ANNIE *demonstrates.*

NATHAN: I shouldn't.

ANNIE: Come on. One won't hurt.

NATHAN: I've never drunk alcohol in my life.

ANNIE: Never? Not even a little bit?

NATHAN: Never.

ANNIE: Not even a little bit?

NATHAN: Nah.

ANNIE: It's no big deal, son. It's just another thing God put on this planet. Fuck, in his day even Jesus didn't mind a bit of goom, so it can't be that bad. Tell you what… we'll flip for it again.

NATHAN: No.

ANNIE: Come on. It's your birthday.

> NATHAN *takes the coin again and flips it. It lands.* ANNIE *sees the result.*
>
> *Sudden snap of memory.*

FAITH: If you walk out that door, God help you, you won't be coming back here. Do you hear me, Annie? Annie? Annie? Annie. You'll never be happy if you leave this island. Do you hear me, you'll never be happy.

♦ ♦ ♦ ♦ ♦

SCENE FIVE: THE PRESENT DAY

ANNIE *is drunk.* NATHAN *is offstage throwing up in a bathroom.*

ANNIE: Maybe you should have eaten something, son.

> NATHAN *enters, cleaning his tie. He's drunk.* ANNIE'*s laughing to herself.*

NATHAN: Maybe I shouldn't have drunk so much, Mum.

ANNIE: You got to learn to hold your liquor, if you want to be a son of mine.

NATHAN: [*looking at his watch*] Oh, fuck.

ANNIE: Ring in sick.

NATHAN: They'll know.

ANNIE: No they won't, I know how to do it.

NATHAN: No I can't.

ANNIE: Give me that thing there… years of practice

> ANNIE *reaches into a pocket for* NATHAN'*s phone.*

NATHAN: [*holding his stomach*] Oh, fuuuuuck… Remind me never to do this again.

ANNIE: Jesus… can this thing give a blow job in the morning too or what?!

NATHAN: Here.

> *He finds the number, presses the buttons and puts the phone to his ear.* ANNIE *tries to get it back.*

No, I better do it.

ANNIE *wrestles the phone back. She speaks with a rather affected poshness.*

ANNIE: [*into the phone*] Hello. Who am I speaking with?... Hello, sir. My name is Sylvia Anne Yeoman, Nathan's mother... Yes... Thank you, yes a sad loss to the family but, you know, you get over that. [*Re-gathering her composure*] I'm ringing on behalf of Nathan, he's very sick at the moment, throwing up and the like. I really don't want to let him go on the barge with such a weak stomach. What, with all the stress and the funeral, I think my little boy's a wee fragile...

She plays with NATHAN*'s hair as she talks.*

Yes, I know. He works so hard. He's such a shining light for our community—but pride cometh before the fall... Sorry... Really?... He didn't tell me that.

NATHAN *tries to take back the phone but* ANNIE *walks out of his reach.*

I know he would really appreciate the time out. He and I have so much to catch up on, years really. Just what the doctor ordered... Thank you so much... Yes, thank you. Maybe one day we should all catch up for a drink, you sound like a lovely man. So forceful and strong or maybe if you left the wife at home...

NATHAN: Annie!

ANNIE: [*into the phone*] Sorry, Nathan needs me. Ta-ta.

She hangs up.

NATHAN: So forceful and strong?

ANNIE: You got to put yourself out there, Nathan. You never know your luck.

NATHAN: You're wasting your time.

ANNIE: Married men are easy.

NATHAN: He bats for my team.

ANNIE: Oh. Fuck, this country's being run by fags?

NATHAN: I don't think two of us constitutes a revolution.

Pause.

NATHAN: [*referring to the telephone call*] You're pretty good at that.

ANNIE: Had practice. That's how I'd survive the week.

NATHAN *looks puzzled.* ANNIE *is buoyant. She pours more drinks.*

He'd wake up on a Monday—doesn't matter who/ could've been any 'He', same pattern every time—it was like so a woman could see the patterns as they happened—like knowing what the weather was going to be before the clouds came in… he'd wake up all hairy and he'd get guilty for getting crook and being on the piss all weekend and there'd be no money/ so he'd get all ready for work and he'd be apologising and saying sorry that he wasn't a good fella to me and the rest/ and off he'd go. And there he'd be, working, shovelling shit or digging holes or cutting up meat or whatever, he'd be a bit green around the gills, see, and them other fellas would smell it on him and they'd know/ and he'd know that they know/ and he'd get shame at first/ then he'd get paranoid. He'd start to sit by hisself and not talk to the other lads and then if he made a mistake or they laughed about it or even if they were just laughing… Well, anyway, I'd pay for it that night. [*Pause.*] So it got to be that, it was better not to have the money. I'd ring up and talk to the boss and so… There.

NATHAN: What would he do?

ANNIE: Don't get all silly on me. Want another drink, son?

NATHAN: No. Thank you.

ANNIE: Go on, have another drink with your mother.

NATHAN: Annie. I said no.

ANNIE: Yes I know, but sometimes no means yes.

NATHAN: Well, this time no means no.

ANNIE *pours two more glasses of Jackie D, emptying the bottle. She slams her drink back and looks at* NATHAN. *She pushes the glass towards him. Finally he takes the glass and slams it back.*

ANNIE: [*smiling*] I'll get us another bottle.

ANNIE *rushes off.*

NATHAN: I know, I know. I'm sorry. She is the devil.

NATHAN *smiles to himself.*

♦ ♦ ♦ ♦ ♦

SCENE SIX: TWO WEEKS AGO

There's a knock at the flywire door.

FAITH: [*offstage*] Come in.

> ANNIE *walks in with a bag full of clothes and stuff. She plonks the bag down on the table.*
>
> FAITH *enters with a tea towel over her shoulder.*
>
> *The two women look at each other.*

I've got no money if that's what you've come back for.

ANNIE: I didn't come for money.

FAITH: You alone?

ANNIE: I'm by myself.

> FAITH *looks at the bag of clothes.*

FAITH: You wanting to stay somewhere?

ANNIE: And it's so good to see you too, Mum.

FAITH: There's Nathan's old room, but you might feel better staying at Martin's down the road.

ANNIE: Yeah, that might be better.

FAITH: How long?

ANNIE: Long enough. I'm in no rush.

FAITH: Always rushing to your grave.

ANNIE: Thinking I might hang here 'til his birthday. Is he coming back?

FAITH: No.

> ANNIE *looks at* FAITH.

FAITH: He had to go to Tokyo this month, he said.

ANNIE: Do you have a photo?

> FAITH *opens a drawer in the table and takes out a photo album. It's jammed full of clippings and photos and ribbons. She opens the album to the final pages and points at a photo.*

FAITH: There he is.

ANNIE: How old is he now?

FAITH: You know when he was born.

ANNIE: Is it thirty-five? Is he tall?

FAITH: Tall enough.

ANNIE: He looks like me, doesn't he... his eyes. He's got good teeth, hasn't he? Handsome.

Silence.

FAITH: I'll make tea.

Silence.

FAITH *brings back the tea things. It's long and tortured.*

ANNIE: I had this dream. I saw you lying flat-out on the table here. As clear as day I saw it, and I couldn't speak... I couldn't say anything... like nothing, nothing, nothing would come out my mouth. And in this dream, [*laughing*] I saw a little tree in your mouth... a seedling... and you were lying there really pale, dressed in your church clothes. And that same next day I got Nathan's letter, asking about his father. I don't know what it means...

FAITH: I haven't told Nathan anything, if that's what you're asking. (Some things are best left unsaid, Annie.)

ANNIE: Those stories you tell... you're always going on about those stories. Why is this one... (any different?) Listen, Old Girl, maybe you're meant to tell them stories, too. The hard ones.

FAITH: No you don't. (You don't come back and muck everything up.) I'm an old woman, I don't want things to be mucked up no more.

ANNIE: Well, what about the rest of us?

FAITH: When I'm gone you do what you want, but I'm not dwelling on the bad things... Those bad stories, you tell them ones and they just keep growing... they eat you up. Better to carry your own burdens and share the happy things, and pray to God to take the bad things away from you.

ANNIE: God?!

FAITH: That's who I am, Annie, and you're never going to change that.

ANNIE: Mumu. I just want to come home. I just want to stay in one place. I don't want to run no more. I can't no more. I'm tired, I got to stop running. I got to stop seeing them bad things... Mumu... I got to come home now. Let me come home now.

FAITH: You know this is your home.

ANNIE: I got to come home. Let me come home. Let me come home, Mumu.

FAITH *takes* ANNIE*'s tears and wipes them into the table.*
Blackout.

♦ ♦ ♦ ♦ ♦

SCENE SEVEN: PRESENT DAY

NATHAN: This is the story of Annie and me.

The story goes something like this... Nana had Annie on this table as soon as she got here... as soon as she'd paid that money for the house her waters broke and she had Annie alone on the table... Nana told the story that she cut the cord herself, lay down for a few minutes and then got up and started cleaning...

ANNIE: Yeah, like we believe that one.

NATHAN: She cleaned away the cobwebs and painted some of the rooms so her daughter could have her own home, here where blackfellas cooked and cleaned for others.

ANNIE: It was a dump then and it's a dump now. Open your eyes, boy.

NATHAN: *I'm* telling this story...

ANNIE: Well, you're only telling her side of it/ okay, okay/ sorry—go ahead.

NATHAN: Where was I?...

ANNIE: Blackfellas cooking and cleaning/ as usual...

NATHAN: And Nana helped rebuild the church and when time came she waved the last mission superintendent off as the barge took him back to the mainland.

ANNIE: [*mumbling*] Waved him off, my arse...

NATHAN: Annie!

ANNIE: Look, I was born three months after Old Girl got here. She had at least one midwife and the first lick of paint this place got was when I was ten...

NATHAN *tries to restart but* ANNIE *gives new details.*

... with leftover paint from the mission... and nothing matched... I was there, I know what it was like.

NATHAN: Doesn't matter, does it?

ANNIE: Go on, you keep yarning, off you go.

NATHAN: So, eventually Nana gets taken to the site where Kawana was buried, down the hill in an unmarked grave. Only the old women knew where it was. She'd died one winter, her heart broken and they'd buried her tribal way, even though she wasn't a 'proper' woman. When Annie was about...

ANNIE: I was seven—when Aunty came back.

NATHAN: When Annie was seven... Hope returned. Nana's eldest sister returned after all those years away. She had made her way back, the eldest coming back not knowing that Nana was her sister, not knowing she had any sisters at all. But when Nana saw her she knew, she knew they belonged together... that they belonged here. They hugged for an hour, crying... and then they talked for three days only stopping to cook meals they remembered and eating at Cookie's Table.

ANNIE: What, they never needed to take a piss?

NATHAN: Three years later—Joy returned and the three sisters talked more and more—but neither of them had children/ neither of them could have children. From one thing or another they could never give birth.

ANNIE: Them doctors stopped them from having children, that's why they couldn't/ those old girls had real pain, they did—real pain.

NATHAN: Nana Joy adopted a boy from the island...

ANNIE: Marty Manager/ womba dickhead.

NATHAN: But she never married. And Nana Hope married Uncle Stevie Salter and moved further up the hill to have a view over all the bay.

ANNIE: That's it, we can stop there now.

NATHAN: Which only leaves *us*—the final part of the family tree. [*Pause.*] Me and the twins and girls' father Ryan Harris, and my father.

ANNIE: Fuck-knuckle...

NATHAN: He had a name...

ANNIE: Yeah, fuck—knuckle, that's all the name he deserves. [*Sobering up really quickly*] I want to stop this shit.

NATHAN: It's not shit. It's the missing bits on the table.

ANNIE: Fuck the table. Fucken take the thing if you want it that much. Fucken take it away, see if I care.

NATHAN: It's the last bits. That's what I want from you, Annie. (That's all I've ever wanted.)

ANNIE: Well, it's not yours to have.

NATHAN: That's what I need from you and then I can go. I just want to know who my father was. I need to know the story of my birth.

ANNIE: [*lying*] I can't remember his name. There, it could have been any one of a dozen boys.

NATHAN: No one tells me anything of what he was like. Did you love him?

ANNIE: [*the answer slips out involuntarily*] No... I was thirteen, for Christ's sake. I didn't know...

NATHAN: Do I look like him?

ANNIE: Finish the fucken story.

NATHAN: I'm trying to.

ANNIE: And the three sisters lived not far from here in houses of sticks and bricks and then Goldilocks comes along and says if you don't let me in I'll huff and puff and...

NATHAN: Nana, would never tell me.

ANNIE: I'll blow your house in. There's the end of the fucken story for you. The wolf's your fucken father.

> ANNIE *laughs.*

NATHAN: Nana Hope never told me... Nana Joy said she didn't know...

ANNIE: Well, of course they didn't tell you.

NATHAN: Who was he?

ANNIE: They didn't know... [*She's lying.*] I was wild back then... Fucken where's Jack?

> NATHAN *has the bottle of Jack Daniels.*

NATHAN: I want to know.

ANNIE: Give it to me.

NATHAN: You can have the table, you can have everything.

ANNIE: Give me the bottle, cunt.

NATHAN: Tell me.

ANNIE: Fuck ya.

NATHAN: *Tell me!*

> ANNIE *grabs* NATHAN's *hand and smashes the bottle onto the table.* NATHAN's *hand is cut badly.*

ANNIE: Fuck. I told you to give it to me.

NATHAN: I'm bleeding.

ANNIE: I didn't do it…

NATHAN: Shit. Get something.

> ANNIE *races off to the kitchen.*

It's fucking everywhere.

> ANNIE *returns with a tea towel.* NATHAN *starts to wipe the blood off the table.*

ANNIE: I've seen worse.

NATHAN: Not on my fucken hand, you never.

ANNIE: You'll live.

> ANNIE *takes the cloth back and calmly wraps his hand.*

NATHAN: It's my right to know.

ANNIE: No, you don't…

NATHAN: You owe me that.

ANNIE: That's my story/ not yours.

NATHAN: It's my story, too.

ANNIE: You've got so used to getting those stories given to you, now you reckon they're all yours. Well, they're not.

NATHAN: We're talking about my father.

> *Pause.* ANNIE *rubs the blood into the table.*

ANNIE: Who do you want your father to be? You want the story of who he was so you can be like him? Or have someone to blame? You got to work out what story you want to *tell*, son. You should work out who's going tell your story when you're gone. Don't go worrying about your father, there was no love in him. Knowing that story won't give you anyone to love. He called me pretty but he never loved me. All those names on Cookie's Table, they're people who loved, that's why they're there. That's why he's not there.

NATHAN: I miss Nana.

> *He starts to cry.*

ANNIE: (Go on son.)

> *She hugs her son.*

When someone dies it's like you get pushed up the queue, you get closer to dying. And it doesn't happen slowly, like you know it's coming… it hits you like a tidal wave. All the things you thought you needed to say just wash away. That's why having kids is so good, it keeps you thinking about the future.

You got to think about the future. Fuck the past. This table don't mean nothing. Fuck, I can't tell whether those stories are true or not. But we all needed that table. Kawana, those old girls... we needed something to pull us back here, but we don't need that no more. This table belongs down the hill there with Old Girl. It's her memories, her past. It should be buried down there with her. We know where we come from. This table ain't our past, our history... we carry that here.

She puts her hand on his chest.

So you can ask me again who your father was and I'll tell you that whole story, but you got to ask yourself if it'll make a difference to who you are. Will it make a difference to how the future will be?

NATHAN: Annie...

ANNIE: I mean, I'll tell you everything but you got to work out what you really want the story to be. The story of the future. Those old girls weren't telling you what the true stories were, they were telling you what they wanted them to be. The stories are about marking out the horizon, about getting the sun to rise another day. You got to make the story of your future, son. Not let the story of the past lead you. Go on. You tell it how you want it to be. You tell me how the future is and I will tell you everything you want to know. Go on.

NATHAN: This is the story of our family tree.

ANNIE: Go on, son.

NATHAN: The story goes something like this... I was born in the hospital on the mainland, a place that was pulled down years ago. I was born there, but I spent most of my time growing up here on the island. This is my home.

ANNIE: The story goes that he travelled the world, he saw sights and brought back stories that he'd tell around the campfire. Stories of big cities and people he'd met and stories that would have people rolling around on the ground laughing or sitting listening to every word.

NATHAN: The story goes that we took the table from the house and dragged it down the hill; down the hill to the old cemetery. We dug a grave and buried the table deep, buried in the family plot near all the family we knew.

The story goes… that from that grave sprung a tree, small at first, almost runt-like, but it grew fast and strong 'til it was soon four people wide with branches that reached to the heavens and roots they say went so far down they held the island together.

ANNIE: In these branches all the children of the island will play. They'll climb to the highest branch and in one direction they will see the buildings of the city across the bay and in the other direction they will see the whales coming up the coast to have their calves. And it's here in this tree, on the highest point on this island, they will know where they belong. They belong here.

NATHAN: And I'll carve names at the base of the tree and tell stories of old times before we bought the island. Before we owned it. Stories passed down to me of people I'd never met. And as that tree grows, the names will get higher and higher, and more and more names would be carved. When I die I will be buried down the hill surrounded by my family. And they will write on my grave stone, 'He belonged here.' That's all I want to say. 'I belong here.'

THE END

GRIFFIN THEATRE COMPANY AND HOTHOUSE THEATRE
PRESENT THE AUSTRALIAN PREMIERE OF

THE STORY OF THE MIRACLES AT
COOKIE'S TABLE
BY WESLEY ENOCH

Cast		Production	
Annie	**Leah Purcell**	Director	**Marion Potts**
Faith	**Roxanne McDonald**	Designer	**Bruce McKinven**
Nathan	**Russell Smith**	Lighting Designer	**Luiz Pampolha**
Young Nathan	**Ben Dennison &**	Composer/Sound Designer	**Brett Collery**
	Blake Herczeg	Production Manager	**Miles Thomas**
		Stage Manager	**Annette Dale**
		Director's Attachment	**Georgina Sutton**
		Production Attachment	**Carissa Simons**
		Cover Photography	**Mark Rogers**

Production Partner

holding redlich

Artistic Partner

H🌀tHouse
·THEATRE·

The Story of the Miracles at Cookie's Table was assisted through HotHouse Theatre's A Month in the Country residential program, funded jointly by Arts NSW and Albury City.

A HotHouse Theatre commission assisted by: Myer Foundation, Arts NSW, Besen Foundation.

Table supplied by Ironwood.

With support from Arts NSW Indigenous Strategic Projects, City of Sydney and Rio Tinto Aboriginal Foundation.

The Story of the Miracles at Cookie's Table was premiered by Griffin Theatre Company and HotHouse Theatre at the SBW Stables Theatre, Sydney, on 15 August 2007.

GRIFFIN
THEATRE COMPANY

THE SBW STABLES
THEATRE

Griffin is Australia's leading new writing theatre. It develops, produces and promotes contemporary Australian theatre texts in a way that is fresh, passionate, challenging and entertaining. Griffin is the only professional theatre company in Sydney entirely dedicated to this work.

Griffin is one of the Australian theatre's great engine rooms. The hit films *Lantana* and *The Boys* began life as plays produced by Griffin and playwright Michael Gow launched his career through Griffin with the premiere productions of *Away* – now Australia's most loved contemporary play – and *Europe*. Many other plays premiered by Griffin are produced regularly throughout Australia and internationally. Many actors have begun their professional careers at Griffin, including Cate Blanchett and Jacqueline McKenzie.

Griffin is a place of good beginnings.

Griffin is the resident theatre company at the historic SBW Stables Theatre and is proud to curate the venue on behalf of its owner, the Seaborn, Broughton and Walford Foundation. In 2007, the theatre will host five Griffin productions as well as four Griffin Stablemates collaborations and other events.

GRIFFIN THEATRE COMPANY
13 Craigend Street, Kings Cross NSW 2011
Phone: 9332 1052
Fax: 9331 1524
Email: info@griffintheatre.com.au
Web: www.griffintheatre.com.au

SBW STABLES THEATRE
10 Nimrod Street, Kings Cross NSW 2011
Bookings: 1300 306 776
or online at
www.griffintheatre.com.au

WESLEY ENOCH
WRITER

Wesley Enoch is the eldest son of Doug and Lyn Enoch, from Stradbroke Island. He has been Resident Director at Sydney Theatre Company, Artistic Director of Kooemba Jdarra Indigenous Performing Arts, and Ilbijerri Aboriginal and Torres Strait Islander Theatre; Associate Artist with Queensland Theatre Company; director of the Indigenous section of the 2006 Commonwealth Games Opening Ceremony; and Associate Artistic Director for Company B. As a writer, his work includes *The Sunshine Club*, *A Life of Grace and Piety*, *Grace*, *The Story of the Miracles at Cookie's Table* (winner of the Patrick White Award 2006). Directing credits include *The Dreamers*, *Conversations with the Dead*, *Capricornia*, *Parramatta Girls*, *Paul* (Company B Belvoir); *Maralinga* (The Australian Nuclear Veterans' Association); *Stolen*, *Black Medea* (Playbox / Malthouse); *The Sunshine Club*, *The Cherry Pickers*, *Black-Ed Up*, *Black Medea*, *The 7 Stages of Grieving* (Sydney Theatre Company); *The Sapphires* (Melbourne Theatre Company); *Black-Ed Up*, *Radiance*, *The Sunshine Club*, *Fountains Beyond* (Queensland Theatre Company); *Murri Love*, *The 7 Stages of Grieving*, *The Dreamers*, *Changing Time*, *Purple Dreams*, *Bitin' Back* (Kooemba Jdarra); *Stolen*, *Shrunken Iris*, *Rainbow's End* and *Headhunter* (Polygot Puppet Theatre / Ilbijerri); *Riverland* (Windmill Performing Arts and Adelaide and Perth International Festivals); and *Eora Crossing* (Legs on the Wall / Sydney Festival).

MARION POTTS
DIRECTOR

Marion's directing credits include *Volpone, Don Juan, Life After George, Beauty Queen of Leenane* (Associate Director, 2000 tour), *Cyrano de Bergerac, The Crucible, Navigating, Del Del, Closer, The Herbal Bed, What Is The Matter With Mary Jane?, Pygmalion, Where Are We Now?* (Playgrounds), *The Café Latte Kid, The Blessing* and *Two Weeks With The Queen* for Sydney Theatre Company; *Equus, The Torrents, Gary's House, A Number* and *The Goat, or, Who Is Sylvia* for State Theatre Company of South Australia. *The Goat* won Marion the Helpmann Award for Best Direction of a Play and was remounted for Company B, Belvoir St. Other credits include *The Popular Mechanicals 1 and 2* (Associate Director) and *The Frogs* (Assistant Director) for Company B, *Big Hair In America* and *Wonderlands* for HotHouse Theatre, *Tales From The Vienna Woods* (NIDA); *Beecham* (Marian St.), and *Dreaming Transportation* for Performing Lines/Opera and The Actors at Work Programme for The Bell Shakespeare Company. Marion was Resident Director for Sydney Theatre Company from 1995–1999 and Artistic Director of Pulse 1997–1999. Marion curated the 2003 National Playwright's Conference and is currently a chairperson of World Interplay, Associate Director at Bell Shakespeare Company and a member of the Theatre Board of the Australia Council and HotHouse Theatre's Artistic Directorate.

ROXANNE McDONALD

Roxanne is a descendant of the Kangoulu, Darambal and Mandandanji tribes of Queensland. Roxanne has worked in theatre since the early 90's and is regarded as one of Brisbane's finest and most versatile actors. This will be Roxanne's first Griffin Theatre production. Her theatre credits include *Parramatta Girls* (Company B); *Radiance* (Kooemba Jdarra/Queensland Theatre Company); *Romeo & Juliet* (Kooemba Jdarra/La Boite Theatre Company); *The Cherry Pickers, Yarnin' Up, Bethel and Maude, A Life of Grace and Piety, Black Shorts, Skin Deep, Seems Like Yesterday, Luck of the Draw, Njunjul the Sun, Changing Time, Spirit, Bitin' Back* (Kooemba Jdarra); *Richard II, The Skin of Our Teeth, The Sunshine Club, Fountains Beyond, Black-ed Up, Brolgas Touring Programs* (Queensland Theatre Company); *Murri Time* (Kite Theatre); *Coriolanus* (Fractal Theatre) and *The Taming of the Shrew* (La Boite Theatre Company). Her film credits include *Grace* and *My Country*. In 2000 Roxanne received a special commendation Matilda Award.

LEAH PURCELL

Leah Purcell is one of Australia's leading actors, with award-winning roles in theatre, film and television. Her first professional break came in 1993 when she was cast in *Bran Nue Dae*, which toured Australia to rave reviews. Her theatre credits include *Parramatta Girls*, *Stuff Happens* (Company B), *The Marriage of Figaro* (Company B/Sydney 2000 Olympic Arts Festival), *The Good Body* (Adelaide Fringe), *Stickybricks*, *Black Chicks Talking* (Sydney Festival and tour), *The Vagina Monologues* (Various), *Beasty Girl: The Secret Life of Errol Flynn*, *Nowhere* (Melbourne Festival). Perhaps Leah's stand out role was in the one-woman show she also co-wrote *Box The Pony*, which has played nationally, at the Edinburgh Arts Festival, in London and in New York. Her film and television credits are also extensive and include *Jindabyne*, *The Proposition*, *Somersault*, *Lantana*, *Water Rats*, *GP*, *Police Rescue* and regular roles in both *Love My Way* and *Fallen Angels*. Leah has also been a presenter, writer, director and music performer and has won a number of awards including the Deadly Award for Actor of the Year in 2005 for *Stuff Happens* and the Green Room Award for Best Actress in a play in 2004 for *Beasty Girl*. This is Leah's first performance with Griffin Theatre.

RUSSELL SMITH

Russell is a graduate of NIDA's Performing Arts degree (2002) and WAAPA's Indigenous Theatre course (1999). Since graduating, Russell has worked as and actor and a director. His credits as an actor include *Seven Pirates*, the national tour of *It's A Dad Thing*, as well as *Acrobats* and *Sleeping Around* in 2004, and *Junction* in 2003. For television, Russell has appeared in a number of guest roles in *Comedy Inc*. While at NIDA he performed in *Cleansed* directed by John Sheedy, *Jarrabin* directed by John Clark, and *Country Music* directed by Tony Knight. Russell made his directorial debut with *No Answer* for NAISDA. Most recently Russell toured regional NSW tutoring acting workshops for Monkey Baa.

BRUCE McKINVEN
DESIGNER

Bruce graduated from QUT's Visual Arts course in 1994 and NIDA's Design course in 1997. Prior to NIDA he was Design Assistant for various Brisbane and Sydney based companies. Set and Costume design credits in theatre include *Othello* [costumes] (Bell Shakespeare Company); *The Dying Gaul* and *Hamlet* [set] (State Theatre Company of South Australia); *Bill & Mary*, *A Conversation*, *The Lonesome West*, *Proof*, *Eating Ice Cream With Your*

Eyes Closed, God is a DJ, Vincent in Brixton, Hitchcock Blonde, A Streetcar Named Desire, American Buffalo, Constance Drinkwater and *Private Fears in Public Places* (Queensland Theatre Company); *Last Drinks* (La Boite) and *Dead Caesar* (Sydney Theatre Company). In dance Bruce has designed for Australian Dance Theatre, Garry Stewart, Expressions Dance Company, WA Ballet, Kate Champion's Force Majeure, Brian Lucas and Clare Dyson. Bruce was Assistant to the Costume Designer for *Snugglepot and Cuddlepie* (Company B and Windmill). For the Adelaide Festival, Bruce has worked in numerous production/design roles from 1994 to 2004. Film credits include *Mission Impossible 2* (Wardrobe Assistant Art Finisher) and *Scooby Doo* (Costume/Props Maker). In 2001, Bruce was awarded The Mike Walsh Fellowship, enabling him to work with Dublin dance company Cois Ceim. Bruce is currently designing Queensland Theatre Company's *Heroes*.

LUIZ PAMPOLHA
LIGHTING DESIGNER

Luiz' lighting credits include: *The Nightwatchman* (Griffin), *Love-Lies-Bleeding* (STC), *Hitler's Daughter, The Prospectors* (Monkey Baa), *Back In Your Box, Boy Overboard, Three Little Fears, This Territory* (ATYP), *Somewhere, Weather* (Q), *Arabian Night* (NIDA), *Half & Half, Blasted, A Number, 7 Blowjobs, Now That Communism Is Dead My Life Feels Empty, Love* (B-Sharp), *Cloud 9, The Illusion, The Mystery of Irma Vep, The Drowned World, Bangers & Mash, The No Chance In Hell Hotel, Bone* (DTC), *Singing The Lonely Heart, The Man Who* (New Theatre), *A Couple of Blaguards* (AMcK), *CODA, danceTank* (SOH), *Capture the Flag, This Blasted Earth, Cu*t Pi, Thrall, Little Boy, Harry's Christmas, Mother Teresa Is Dead, Tragedy: a tragedy, The Suitors, Constance Drinkwater* (TRS). Luiz, a Sydney Theatre Critics Award Nominee in 2006, is a NIDA graduate and has also designed and co-designed productions for the Edinburgh Fringe, Adelaide Fringe, Belfast and Melbourne International Arts Festivals.

BRETT COLLERY
COMPOSER / SOUND DESIGNER

Brett is a composer and sound designer. His most recent work includes the Queensland Theatre Company productions *Hamlet, The Woman Before, The Estimator, Constance Drinkwater and the Final Days of Somerset, American Buffalo, Away, The Goat, or Who is Sylvia?, Vincent in Brixton, Mano Nera, Eating Ice Cream with Your Eyes Closed, Proof* and *God is a DJ*. Other QTC production include *Phedra, The Messiah, Bill and Mary, Molly Sweeney,*

The Tragedy of King Richard III [co-production with Bell Shakespeare], The Tragedy of King Richard II, The Forest, Top Dogs and Shopping and F$$$ing. Dance credits include collaborative works with choreographer/dance artist Brian Lucas, Underbelly, Monster, The Book of Revelations and Here Then There Now (Brisbane Powerhouse), Fugu San and Rodin's Kiss with Lisa Oneil, Reading Light Illuminating Text with John Utans and Absence[s] with Clare Dyson. Other theatre/performance credits include: The Story of the Miracles at Cookie's Table (Kaze Theatre Tokyo); Bitin' Back, Purple Dreams, Seems Like Yesterday, Going to the Island and Binny's Backyard (Kooemba Jdarra); The Red Tree, Pianissimo (QPAC), Speaking in Tongues (La Boite) plus a myriad of works with local independent artists and organisations including SBS Television, ABC Television, Education Queensland, Southbank Corporation, Triple J, Brisbane Cabaret Festival, and Qld Pride Festival. Film and television soundtracks include Elvis Lives in Parkes, Rubber Gloves, The Truth About Dragonhall, Escape from the Planet of the Tapes and Two Roads to Helidon. He has also performed and recorded with the bands Isis, Gota Cola, Silver Circus and Spiral I. Brett was recently awarded a Gold Matilda Award for Sound Design and has received and been nominated for Helpmann Awards, 4MBS Awards and the Australian Screen Composer Awards.

MILES THOMAS
PRODUCTION MANAGER

This is Miles' third show as Production Manager for Griffin, following on from The Nightwatchman by Daniel Keene and October by Ian Wilding earlier this year. Most recently he has been production coordinator for the Paris Opera Ballet's Sydney tour. He has previously worked in a wide range of production roles for shows including Woomera and Woyzeck at the Old Fitzroy and Into the Woods (SUDS). Over the past few years he has also worked as a regular venue and lighting technician for Sydney Theatre Company, Seymour Centre and the Capitol Theatre.

ANNETTE DALE
STAGE MANAGER

Annette's career in stage management spans 20 years taking her all over Australia and around the world. She has stage managed everything from dance, theatre & events to cabaret, parades and dance parties. Her highlights include Sydney 2000 Olympic and Paralympic Games where she was Presentation Manager for the archery, and her many productions with Chunky Move. Annette last worked with Griffin in 1991.

Leah Purcell (Annie) in rehearsals for Griffin Theatre Company / HotHouse Theatre's production in 2007. Photo by Olivia Martin-McGuire.

Marion Potts (Director) in rehearsals for Griffin Theatre Company / HotHouse Theatre's production in 2007. Photo by Olivia Martin-McGuire.

Roxanne McDonald (Faith) in rehearsals for Griffin Theatre Company / HotHouse Theatre's production in 2007. Photo by Olivia Martin-McGuire.

Russell Smith (Nathan) in rehearsals for Griffin Theatre Company / HotHouse Theatre's production in 2007. Photo by Olivia Martin-McGuire.

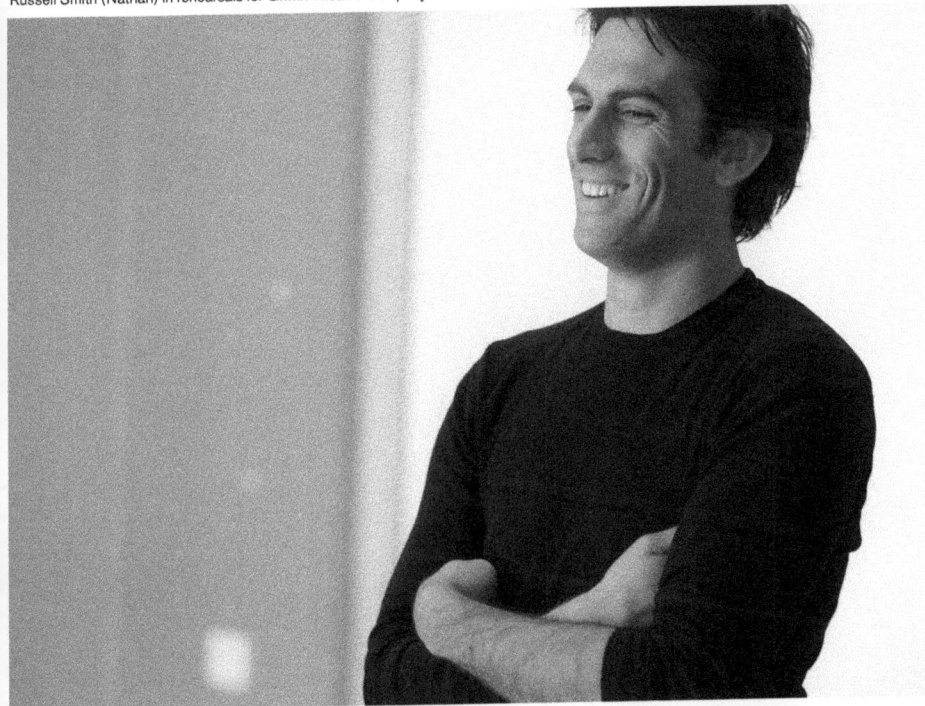

GRIFFIN THEATRE COMPANY

GRIFFIN DONORS

Income from Griffin activities covers less than 50% of Griffin's operating costs – leaving an ever increasing gap for us to fill through government funding, sponsorship and philanthropy. Your support helps us bridge the gap and keep ticket prices affordable and our programs working at their best. To make a donation contact Griffin on 9332 1052 or donate online on the Griffin website www.griffintheatre.com.au

2007 GRIFFIN PARTNERS

Principal Sponsor

PKF
Chartered Accountants
& Business Advisers

Opportunity Partner

gadens
lawyers

Production Partner

holding
redlich

Company Partners

Cornwall STODART
LAWYERS

CURRENCY PRESS
The performing arts publisher
www.currency.com.au

THE FEAROCIOUS FEED

fullcream
media

Harman
Computer
Services

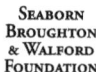

REGENTS
COURT
HOTEL

SEABORN
BROUGHTON
& WALFORD
FOUNDATION

SIGNWAVE
NEWTOWN

TYRRELL'S WINES

UNSW

Artistic Partners

HotHouse
THEATRE

MARDI GRAS
2007
gaydar.com.au

Philanthropic Partners

The
Copyright
Agency Ltd

RIO TINTO
Aboriginal
Fund

THE
MALCOLM ROBERTSON
FOUNDATION

Honorary Auditors

Rosenfeld,
Kant & Co.

SBW Stables Theatre Owned By

SBW
Foundation
SEABORN BROUGHTON WALFORD
FOUNDATION

Government Partners

Australian Government

Australia Council
for the Arts

arts nsw

CITY OF SYDNEY

Griffin Theatre is assisted by the Commonwealth Government through the Australia Council, its arts funding and advisory body; and the NSW Government through Arts NSW.

Griffin acknowledges the generosity of the Seaborn Broughton and Walford Foundation in allowing it, since 1986, the use of the theatre rent free, less outgoings.

HⓄtHouse
·THEATRE·

HOTHOUSE THEATRE, GATEWAY ISLAND, WODONGA
P. O. Box 479, Wodonga, VIC. 3689
Phone: 02 6021 7433   Fax: 02 6023 2201
info@hothousetheatre.com.au
www.hothousetheatre.com.au

**THE HUME BUILDING SOCIETY
BUTTER FACTORY THEATRE WODONGA**
Gateway Island, Wodonga
The Performance Home of HotHouse Theatre

ARTISTIC DIRECTORATE:

Campion Decent, Aidan Fennessy, Tom Healey,
Catherine Jones, Jane Longhurst, Jean-Marc Russ

STAFF:

Campion Decent	Artistic Manager
Bernadette Haldane	General Manager

Administration:

Fiona Elliott	Administrator
Heather Broadfoot	Marketing Manager
Wendy Rose	Administrative Assistant
Charmaine Stephani	Business Development Consultant
Hayley Atkins	Administrative/Venue Assistant
Mavis Ford	Development Coordinator
Sebastien Pasche	Drama School Coordinator

Venue & Technical:

Rob Scott	Technical Manager
Bethwynn Hackett	Venue Manager
Rebecca Bennell	Production Manager
Jason Glass	Technical Trainee

BOARD OF DIRECTORS:

Bill Robbins (Chair), Gudrun Reid (Deputy Chair), John Baker,
Carol Drummond, John Gunson, Lisa Mahood, Di Thomas,
Prof. David Throsby, Les Tomich, Fiona Elliott

HotHouse Theatre - A Regional Voice on the National Stage

H⊚tHouse
·T H E A T R E·

As one of Australia's oldest professional, regionally based theatre companies HotHouse Theatre has made a significant contribution to the Australian performing arts industry and is fundamental to the cultural vitality of Albury/Wodonga.

HotHouse Theatre is the leading regional theatre company in Australia. As an integral part of the fabric of the local community, it has a long and proud history underpinned by the company's commitment to remain at the fore of artistic excellence in contemporary performing arts practice.

Each year HotHouse presents the very best theatre from the local, national and international stages. HotHouse Theatre also commissions new work from leading Australian playwrights, runs an extensive training program, tours regionally and nationally, operates the Hume Building Society Butter Factory Theatre Wodonga on behalf of the City of Wodonga, and facilitates the national creative development program *A Month in the Country* funded jointly by AlburyCity, Arts NSW and The Myer Foundation.

---

arts|nsw   ARTS VICTORIA   Victoria The Place To Be   Australian Government   O Australia Council for the Arts

CITY OF WODONGA VIC   VicHealth ARTS FOR HEALTH   AlburyCity

The Story of the Miracles at Cookie's Table was commissioned by HotHouse Theatre, assisted by:

arts|nsw   Besen Family FOUNDATION   THE MYER FOUNDATION   NMF NELSON MEERS FOUNDATION

The Story of the Miracles at Cookie's Table was assisted through HotHouse Theatre's A Month in the Country residential program, funded jointly by Arts NSW and AlburyCity.

www.ingramcontent.com/pod-product-compliance
Lightning Source LLC
Chambersburg PA
CBHW041933090426
42744CB00017B/2034